高等学校
英语应用能力考试（口试）
实训教程

主　　编　屈赛英　晏书红
副 主 编　周　珊　李桂红　程萍萍
参编人员　郝连春　苟锦毅　陈　莉
　　　　　王　巧　严礼山

北京理工大学出版社
BEIJING INSTITUTE OF TECHNOLOGY PRESS

版权专有　侵权必究

图书在版编目（CIP）数据

高等学校英语应用能力考试（口试）实训教程 / 屈赛英，晏书红主编. --北京：北京理工大学出版社，2021.9
　　ISBN 978-7-5763-0310-0

Ⅰ．①高… Ⅱ．①屈… ②晏… Ⅲ．①大学英语水平考试-口语-教材 Ⅳ．①H319.9

中国版本图书馆 CIP 数据核字（2021）第 184701 号

出版发行 /	北京理工大学出版社有限责任公司
社　　址 /	北京市海淀区中关村南大街 5 号
邮　　编 /	100081
电　　话 /	（010）68914775（总编室）
	（010）82562903（教材售后服务热线）
	（010）68944723（其他图书服务热线）
网　　址 /	http://www.bitpress.com.cn
经　　销 /	全国各地新华书店
印　　刷 /	三河市天利华印刷装订有限公司
开　　本 /	787 毫米×1092 毫米　1/16
印　　张 /	12.25
字　　数 /	208 千字
版　　次 /	2021 年 9 月第 1 版　2021 年 9 月第 1 次印刷
定　　价 /	39.00 元

责任编辑 / 武丽娟
文案编辑 / 把明宇
责任校对 / 周瑞红
责任印制 / 施胜娟

图书出现印装质量问题，请拨打售后服务热线，本社负责调换

编写委员会

主　任：史宝凤

副主任：张　琦　徐宏俊　姚月霞

顾　问：刘晓林

委　员：（按照姓氏笔画排序）

王克林　王海舟　仲菊芳　刘　芳　祁丛林

孙丽丽　孙洪泉　孙淑萍　纪忠杰　吴海华

宋应杰　张　盛　张立图　陈偶娣　罗　纯

季国华　屈赛英　赵　朵　夏　勤　徐意雯

曹加文　梁文亮　程显毅　薛胜军　戴国梅

总　序

教材亦即课本，是根据教学大纲和实际需要，为师生教学应用而编选的材料，有教科书、讲义、讲授提纲等不同形式。这种依据课程标准编制的、系统反映学科内容的教学用书，是课程标准的具体化，是体现国家意志，是解决为谁培养人、培养什么人、怎样培养人这一根本问题的载体。新时代的教材不仅要始终坚持正确的政治方向和价值导向，而且要紧扣学校人才培养目标，以学生为本，注重学生的兴趣、能力和社会的需要，按照有关科学知识的内在逻辑顺序组织教材，依法依规推进教材建设。这不仅是新时代的需要，也是党的教育方针的要求，亦是硅湖职业技术学院推进"立德树人、产学一体，培养具有创新创业精神和能力的高素质技术技能人才"的"一体两翼"发展战略。

"一体两翼"人才培养模式改革，旨在培养产教融合创新创业人才，并在全院推行完全学分制的教学改革的基础上，形成了"烙印课""平台课""校企合作课""创新创业课""课程思政示范课"五位一体的硅湖特色课程体系；把知识点重组后的教学内容通过教材的形式固化，将"人工智能""创新创业"等学科前沿理念贯穿于高等职业教育系列教材。这不仅是学校的教学改革成果，更是学校响应国务院《国家职业教育深化改革实施方案》（"职教20条"）中强调"校企双元"合作开发教材的要求，从而全面贯彻教育部《职业院校教材管理办法》（教材〔2019〕3号）相关规定，达到由院内自编教材为起点，分阶段逐步打造具有"活页式+资源库"特色的新型正式出版教材的终极目的。基于此，学院计划自2020年起，用3～5年的时间着力打造一批产教深度融合、校企共同开发、具有"硅湖"特色的校级系列规划教材。

我们希望该系列教材既要结合区域专业职业岗位要求，符合地区行业发展，又要结合使用人群学习能力实际情况；内容要科学、合理，既要符合学生认知规律，也要符合行业操作规范，还要适合实际岗位需求，更要适应社会发展行业更替的需要。

硅湖职业技术学院教材编写委员会
二〇二一年七月五日

Preface 前言

  高等学校英语应用能力考试（口试）适用于达到高职教育英语课程基础要求的高等职业教育、普通高职高专教育的非英语专业的学生，目的是考核学生的英语基础知识和语言技能，以及使用英语进行日常的涉外交际与业务交际的能力。

  高等学校英语应用能力考试（口试）经过多年的试测，已逐步臻于成熟。其进一步试行和推广不仅对高职高专英语教学坚持走实用英语的方向具有重要意义，也一定会有利于用人单位了解高职人才的涉外口头交际能力，同时更好更多地聘用高水平的高职高专毕业生。为了强化学生英语应用能力，帮助学生进一步熟悉口试的题型和内容，助力学生顺利通过考试，我们编写了《高等学校英语应用能力考试（口试）实训教程》一书。

  全书分为四大部分：①考试大纲；②具体单元内容；③口试考试样题；④补充对话。

  目前高职院校基础英语课时相对压缩，所以培养学生自主学习能力尤为重要。本书介绍了考试大纲，反复操练考试考点，让学生有机会充分锻炼考试技巧。学生在进行全真模拟训练时能得到同步实战训练。本书具有较高的备考训练价值。

  本书由硅湖职业技术学院英语教研室的教师编写。编者均来自高职院校教学一线，拥有多年的英语教学经验。由于编写时间仓促，加之编者水平有限，书中存在的不足与疏漏之处在所难免，望同行和读者批评指正。

  最后祝广大考生学习进步，考试成功！

编　者
2021 年 9 月

Contents 目录

第一部分　全国《高等学校英语应用能力考试》口试大纲　1

全国《高等学校英语应用能力考试》口试大纲

——高等学校英语应用能力考试委员会　3

第二部分　正文　9

Unit 1　Making a Self-introduction　11
- Part 1　Reading Aloud　13
- Part 2　Questions & Answers　14
- Part 3　Chinese-English Interpretation　17
- Part 4　Presentation　18

Unit 2　Talking about Movies　29
- Part 1　Reading Aloud　31
- Part 2　Questions & Answers　32
- Part 3　Chinese-English Interpretation　35
- Part 4　Presentation　36

Unit 3　Seeing a Doctor　47
- Part 1　Reading Aloud　49
- Part 2　Questions & Answers　51
- Part 3　Chinese-English Interpretation　54
- Part 4　Presentation　56

Unit 4　Having an Interview　69
- Part 1　Reading Aloud　71
- Part 2　Questions & Answers　72
- Part 3　Chinese-English Interpretation　74
- Part 4　Presentation　75

Unit 5　Making a Reservation	85
Part 1　Reading Aloud	87
Part 2　Questions & Answers	88
Part 3　Chinese-English Interpretation	90
Part 4　Presentation	91

Unit 6　Visiting a Company	101
Part 1　Reading Aloud	103
Part 2　Questions & Answers	104
Part 3　Chinese-English Interpretation	107
Part 4　Presentation	108

Unit 7　Vacation	115
Part 1　Reading Aloud	117
Part 2　Questions & Answers	118
Part 3　Chinese-English Interpretation	120
Part 4　Presentation	121

Unit 8　The Graduation Ceremony	131
Part 1　Reading Aloud	133
Part 2　Questions & Answers	134
Part 3　Chinese-English Interpretation	137
Part 4　Presentation	138

第三部分　高等学校英语应用能力考试（口试）样题 ································ 151

第四部分　口语补充对话 ································ 161

第一部分

全国《高等学校英语应用能力考试》口试大纲

全国《高等学校英语应用能力考试》口试大纲

——高等学校英语应用能力考试委员会

本考试是"高等学校英语应用能力考试"附设的口语能力考试，由高等学校英语应用能力考试委员会设计、命题和提供评分标准，由各省、市教育主管部门主持、管理和实施。

一、考试简介

（一）考试对象和报考条件

"高等学校英语应用能力考试口语考试"（以下简称"口试"）的报考对象是在校的高职高专学生。

（二）考试形式

口试采用计算机辅助形式，在多媒体教室进行。根据多媒体教室的大小，每场考试可以有数十名考生同时参加。

考试不设主考，只设监考，试题（包括其指示说明）全部集成在本口语考试专用的软件系统中。考生根据软件系统屏幕、语音提示和所给问题，直接以口头方式回答，并通过麦克风实时录制到系统中。

整个考试过程约为 17 分钟，实际考试的时间为 13 到 15 分钟；考生回答问题的实际时间累计约为 7 分钟。

在正式考试开始之前，考生有 1 分 30 秒回答"热身"问题，目的是让考生熟悉、适应考场环境和考试方式，消除考生的紧张感，帮助他们进入良好的应考状态。其内容包括核实考生身份（由考生通过麦克风把自己的姓名和准考证号录入系统中），并让考生回答 3 个问题（如天气、家庭、个人兴趣、校园生活等）。在考生回答完"热身"问题之后，系统提示考生考试正式开始。

考试主体共由 4 个部分组成，各部分之间都有系统提示，提醒考生即将进入下一个部分的考试。

第一部分是朗读短文（Loud Reading），共 1 题，短文长度在 120 词左右。主要测试考生的语音、语调、断句等朗读技巧和流利程度。朗读的材料选自口语体短文或独白，属于口头交际范畴，如开场白、电话转述、口头通知等。考生有 1 分钟的准备时间。在听到系统提示后，考生开始朗读短文，时间为 1 分钟。

第二部分是提问—回答（Questions & Answers）。主要测试考生就交际话题提出问题或给予回应的能力。在这一部分，考生将读到一段实用性的涉外交际活动文字，如广告、启事、通知等。本部分包含两个子部分：提问部分和回答部分。在提问部分，系统将给考生提供一个身份以及所需要完成的任务。根据系统提示的要求，考生需就文字材料内容提出若干问题。在回答部分，系统提示将给考生提供另外一个身份；同时，考生会听到一段内容不完整的对话。考生要根据文字材料内容和所扮演的角色补全该对话。例如，在第一部分，考生先在文字材料中读到一则宾馆的广告，然后录音的第一部分提示：假定考生是一名想要预订房间的顾客。考生需要根据他（她）所看到的广告内容提出若干问题，从而决定他（她）是否要预订房间。在录音的第二部分中，系统提示考生的身份是一个旅行社的职员，需要就顾客的咨询做出恰当的回答。考生在听到系统提示之后应立即开始提问或回答。每一次提问或回答的时间为 10 秒钟。答题时间总计为 1 分钟。

第三部分是汉译英（Chinese-English Interpretation），共 5 题。主要测试考生在日常涉外活动和涉外业务中的口头翻译能力。考生在听到系统提示之后应立即开始或停止口头翻译。实际翻译时间总计为 1 分 40 秒。本部分有以下几种不同的题型：

① 在这一部分的指示说明结束之后，考生将依次听到并口头翻译 5 个不很复杂的中文单句；

② 考生在电脑屏幕上读到一个包含 5 个不很复杂的中文单句的段落。考生有 30 秒钟时间阅读该材料。之后，考生需要将该段落逐句口头翻译成英文；

③ 考生在电脑屏幕上读到一段中英文相间的对话。考生有 30 秒钟时间阅读该对话。然后考生需根据对话所提供的上下文，将对话中的中文部分（共 5 句）口头翻译成英文；

④ 首先，系统将播放一段中英文相间的对话（不显示录音文字），让考生了解该对话的主题以及大致意思。然后，系统将该对话逐句再播放一遍，要求考生将对话中的中文部分（共 5 句）在留出的时间内口头译成英文。

第四部分是看图讲话（Presentation），共 1 题。主要测试考生用英语进行连贯口头表达的能力。在这一部分的指示说明结束之后，考生将在电视屏幕上看到一幅或几幅图片、照片或一个图表（包括简明文字提示），内容涉及广告、产品/公司介绍、信息发布、业务交流等涉外业务交际。考生有 1 分钟时间进行准备。在听到系统提示后，考生需对图片、照片或图表的内容进行连贯陈述。答题时间为 2 分钟。

（三）考试内容

1　语言交际范围

口试要求考生能在不同场景下参与不同形式的口头交际。考生的语言能力将根据他们在考试中的表现进行测定。考生需要掌握的语言交际能力，以《高职高专教育英语课程教学基本要求》交际范围表为依据，包括：

1.1　日常交际：

a. 交际功能：介绍、问候、感谢、致歉、道别、指点、接受、拒绝、问讯等。

b. 交际主题：天气、学习、爱好、饮食、健康、问路等。

1.2　业务交际：

a. 日常涉外活动：迎送，安排日程与活动，安排住宿，宴请与迎送会，陪同外宾购物、游览、就诊等。

b. 一般涉外业务：

* 介绍公司/工厂：历史、现状；

* 介绍产品：类型、性能、规格、市场等；

* 业务洽谈：合作意向、投资意向、签订合同、人员培训、专家待遇、议价、折扣、佣金、订购、付款方式、交货日期、保险等；

* 参加业务交流。

2　系统提供给考生的信息

口试主要以下列三种形式向考生提供考试提示：

2.1　文字提示；

2.2　声音提示；

2.3　画面提示（如图片、图表、动画或录像片段等）。

（四）评分标准及评分描述

口试的评分围绕内容、表达及所用语言等方面，采取在分项评分的基础上总体计分的办法。由考试委员会制定并提供评分细则和评分标准。

（五）成绩与证书

口试成绩分为优秀、合格、不合格三个等级。

优秀：能用英语比较顺利地进行不十分复杂的、一定范围内的日常和业务口头涉外交际。

合格：能用英语进行简单的、一定范围内的日常和业务口头涉外交际。

不合格：尚不具备用英语进行口头交际的能力。

口试成绩合格者，将获得"高等学校英语应用能力考试（口试）"证书。证书分为两个等级：优秀和合格。

（六）考试时间

每年举行一或二次。

（七）考点设置

口试以学校为单位设立考点。达到施考条件的学校向所在省（市）教学主管部门提出申请，经省（市）教学主管部门和高等学校英语应用能力考试委员会协商后确定。考点原则上接受本校的考生报名；有条件的学校可接受外校考生报名。

二、考生须知

（一）考生报名

考生原则上应在设有考点的本学校报名参加考试。跨校报名需得到所报考点的同意。

（二）注意事项

* 考生需携带本人的准考证和身份证准时到规定的候考室报到，逾时 10 分钟即不得进入候考室。此外，在候考期间未经同意不得擅自离开候考室。
* 考试时，考生不得携带任何未经允许的物品（如手机、IPAD、电子词典、收音机和含有存储功能和发声功能的设备器材等），并不得佩戴会发声的饰物。
* 考试期间，考生必须遵守考场纪律，服从监考人员安排。
* 考生不得擅自操作电脑设备。

* 考生应按照系统提示逐项完成任务。每项任务都有规定的准备时间和答录时间。若考生在规定的时间内提前完成任务，须安静地等待系统提出下面一项任务的提示，不得擅离座位。

* 考试实录过程中，考生要适当控制声音的高低，保证录音清晰可辨，否则将会影响考试成绩。

* 如果没有特殊原因，考试一旦开始将不得中途停顿。考生若无故中途退场，将作自动放弃考试处理；该考生已经完成的部分也将视作无效。

* 考试结束后，考生必须根据监考人员要求立即离开考区。

（三）考生培训

考生在报名时，可以自愿购买《高等学校英语应用能力考试（口试）大纲和样题》和《高等学校英语应用能力考试口试指南》，了解考试内容及其形式。在考生报名结束后，各个考点将适时集中公布考生所在考场及候考室等考试安排，并根据需要对考生进行必要的考务培训。

（引用自"百度百科"）

第二部分

正 文

Unit 1

Making a Self-introduction

Warming-up

A. Match the following words with the corresponding pictures:

| freshman   self   introduction   evening party   hilarious   diagram   bar chart |

1. _____

2. _____

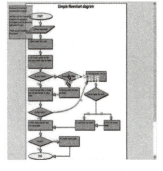

3. _____

4. _____

5. _____

6. _____

B. Use the above words to complete the following sentences:

1. The show was _____ and I couldn't stop laughing.
2. I'm a _____ at Silicon Lake College.
3. In this case, I'm specifying the chart type as a _____.
4. This is, I think, the most famous _____ in all of the financial theories.
5. It is a great honour to be with you at this _____ .
6. Now I'm going to give a brief _____ .

Unit 1

 Part 1　Reading Aloud

Task: Read the following passage aloud

Good Morning, my name is Wang Lili. It is a great honour to have this opportunity to introduce myself. I am a 18-year-old girl, born in Wuxi, Jiangsu province. I am currently a freshman student at Silicon Lake College, and my major is business management.

Generally speaking, I am a hard-working student especially when I do things I am interested in. And I am optimistic and confident. Sometimes I prefer to stay alone, reading and listening to music. In my spare time, I often go shopping with my friends, surf on the internet and also do some sports, such as running and roller-skating.

I love English very much and I hope I can make a rapid progress in the following years in English. This is my brief introduction. Thank you for your kind attention.

Examine Tips

When reading English, we should pay attention to the following matters and master the relevant skills：
- Pronunciation should be standard;
- The voice should be in cadence, high when the high, light when the light;
- Pay attention to the pauses in reading

Part 2 Questions & Answers

Task One

Suppose you want to participate in the party. Read the following poster and you are required to ask 3 questions for detailed information.

Welcome to Join our Evening Party

Theme: Evening Party for Welcoming the New Arrivals
Participants: <u>Question 1</u>
Time: <u>Question 2</u>
Place: <u>Question 3</u>
Content: Songs, dancing, games and so on.
Contact Person: Linda Wang
Telephone Number: 57788001

Useful questions:

- Ask the place:

    Where will the event be held?
    Where is the location of the company?
    What is the address of the hotel?

- Ask people:

    Who will attend the conference?
    Who will be invited to take part in the competition?

- Ask the time:

    When will the party begin?
    What time will the job fair start?

Unit 1

- Ask the price:

  How much is the new model of smart phone?
  What is the price of the tour package?

- Ask for the contact information:

  How can I contact the person?
  What is the telephone number?
  What is the website of the company?

Task Two

Based on the same poster for the evening party, read the following dialogue between two friends, Wang Lili(W) and Li Lei(L). Suppose you are Li Lei, while reading, you are required to complete the conversation by answering Wang Lili's questions.

Welcome to Join our Evening Party

Theme: Evening Party for Welcoming the New Arrivals
Participants: all the students
Time: Sept.15, 2020
Place: Student Center
Content: Songs, dancing, games and so on.
Contact Person: Linda Wang
Telephone Number: 57788001

W: Hi Li Lei. What's new? You look so happy.

L: Hi Wang Lili. Nice to see you. I've just read the poster for evening party for welcoming the new arrivals. It seems there are lots of programs, such as songs, dancing, and games.

W: Really? When and where?

L: _____.

W: But who will be invited to join the party?

L: _____.

W: That's nice. Would you like to join it?

L: Of course. I am a hilarious person as you know. How about you? Will you join me?

W: I'd love to but unfortunately I have another appointment on that day.

L: What a pity! Anyway I hope we can meet at next party.

W: Sure. Hope you can have fun at the party.

Examine Tips

- When answering a question, pay attention to the special interrogative pronoun or special interrogative adverb of the question, find the corresponding text content in the notice, and make a correct answer;
- The expression of information such as telephone number or address: cannot read the number in Chinese;
- The expression of the website: in the website, for ".", it should be pronounced "dot" instead of "dian" in Chinese. For example, www.usl.edu.cn, it should be pronounced "WWW dot usl dot edu dot cn".

Part 3 Chinese-English Interpretation

Task: In this part, you are required to translate a short speech into English orally.

大家好！我的名字是李雷，很高兴有机会在这里做自我介绍。我今年18岁，来自江苏苏州。目前是硅湖职业技术学院的一名大一新生，我的专业是计算机网络技术。

至于我的个性特点，总的来说就是活泼好动，外向开朗。我有很多爱好，比如篮球、跑步、游泳等。我还在中学得过1 500米跑步比赛第一名，我以此为傲。

来到硅湖开始我的大学生活，我期待在自己的学业上取得优良成绩。谢谢大家！

Useful sentences for self-introduction：

- Hello. My name is Amy. I am from New York. I am an accountant. I work in a telephone company.
- I am Nicola. I work as a receptionist in a construction company. I like my job very much. My hobbies are reading and painting. I also love reading novels.
- My name is Richard. I am 27. I am a sales manager. I work for a company that imports electric motors from China. I travel a lot for business, but I like to travel so it is fun.

Part 4 Presentation

Task: In this part, you are required to talk about what is shown in the following diagram, describing and summarizing its contents. You should add your own comments.

Survey about the purpose of surfing online for college students

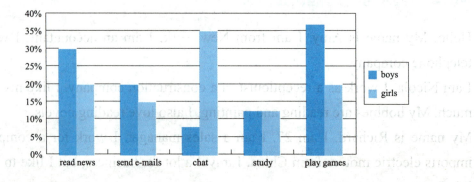

Useful sentences patterns:

● At the beginning:

1. As can be seen from the chart/graph/table...
2. It can be seen from the statistics that...

3. The chart gives information that...

• while describing:

1. There was a rise/increase/upward trend from...to...
2. It has risen to an average of...
3. There was a fall/decrease/reduction/decline/drop/downward trend from...to...

• At the end:

1. From the analyses above, we can draw the conclusion that...
2. From the data we gathered from the above graph, we can conclude that...
3. According to the information gathered above, we may reach the conclusion that...
4. According to what has been discussed above, we can arrive at the conclusion that...
5. The graph reflects that...

Practice after the unit

Exercise 1 Ask questions about the underlined parts:

1. He is <u>my father</u>.

2. They are <u>under the tree</u>.

3. I often watch TV <u>after dinner</u>.

4. Lily swims <u>in the swimming pool</u>.

5. I often brush my teeth <u>in the evening</u>.

6. <u>Alan</u> likes to play with Bill.

Exercise 2 Translate the following sentences into English:

1. 大家好！很荣幸在这里做一个自我介绍。

2. 我爱好英语、读书，也喜欢户外活动，比如打篮球、慢跑等。

3. 我给自己大学期间设定的小目标是，学好专业课程并顺利通过英语四级考试。

4. 这幅图表对比了两家公司在 2010 年至 2015 年雇员人数的变化情况。

5. 正如以上柱状图中所看到的，我校的招生人数从 2017 年至 2020 年连续三年保持稳步上升趋势。

6. 从以上分析，我们可以得出结论，超过半数的人更愿意通过招聘会方式找到自己心仪的工作。

Words List

1. opportunity [ˌɒpə'tjuːnəti]   n.   时机，机会
2. currently ['kʌrəntli]   adv.   当前；一般地
3. major ['meɪdʒə(r)]   n.   专业；主修
4. optimistic [ˌɒptɪ'mɪstɪk]   adj.   乐观的；乐观主义的
5. roller-skating ['roʊlər skeɪtɪŋ]   n.   轮式溜冰；滑旱冰
6. arrival [ə'raɪvl]   n.   到来；到达；到达者
7. event [ɪ'vent]   n.   事件；活动；大事；体育项目
8. hilarious [hɪ'leəriəs]   adj.   欢闹的；非常滑稽的；喜不自禁的
9. unfortunately [ʌn'fɔːtʃənətli]   adv.   可惜；很遗憾；不幸的是
10. appointment [ə'pɔɪntmənt]   n.   约会；预约；任命

Unit 1

Reference answers

Part 2

Task One

    Question 1   Who will be invited to participate the evening party?

    Question 2   When will the evening party start?

    Question 3   Where will the evening party be held?

Task Two

    The evening party will be held at Student Center on September 15, 2020.

    All the students are welcome to join the party.

Part 3

    Hello everyone! My name is Li Lei. I'm glad to have the opportunity to introduce myself here. I am 18 years old, from Suzhou, Jiangsu Province. At present, I am a freshman in Silicon Lake Vocational and Technical College. My major is computer network technology.

    As for my personality, generally speaking, I am lively and outgoing. I have many hobbies, such as basketball, running, swimming and so on. I also won the first place in the 1500 meter running competition in middle school. I'm proud of it.

    I came to silicon lake to start my college life. I am looking forward to getting good grades in my studies. Thank you!

Part 4

    Nowadays surfing the internet is very popular on campus. As can be seen from the above bar chat, many college students, boys and girls, spend much more time playing games and chatting on the internet. However, as for the purpose of surfing online for the college students, there are many different characteristics between boys and girls.

Based on the survey, there are 35% of girls surfing online for chatting while the number of boys only accounts for less than 10%; However, more than 35% of boys focus on playing games on the internet, while only 20% of girls like games online; Compared to girls, more boys use internet to read news and send emails, which the proportion is 30% and 20% respectively. And while using internet for the purpose of study, the percent for boys and girls is the same, which is only 12%.

According to the information gathered above, we may reach the conclusion that both boys and girls on campus surf online most for the purpose of entertainment. So in my opinion, college students should deal with the internet carefully. On the one hand, we can get some pleasure and knowledge. On the another hand, we shouldn't spend too much time, energy and money on the internet because study is the priority. In conclusion, we should make good and proper use of the internet.

Unit 1

Bilingual Reading Time

It may be time to adopt Asian greetings
也许到了该采用亚洲式问候礼的时候了

Now, with the novel coronavirus spreading around the world, customs are starting to change. With the virus' spread becoming more serious in Western countries, recommendations to forgo embrace and handshake as well as the customary greeting kiss are seen by some as an overreaction. People don't want to give up cherished social customs, even if there are risks.

现在，随着新型冠状病毒在世界范围内的传播，习俗开始发生变化。随着病毒在西方国家的传播变得愈加严重，放弃拥抱和握手以及习惯性的问候之吻的建议被认为是一种过度反应。即使存在风险，人们也不想放弃珍贵的社会风俗。

Still, times are changing. Various forms of greeting like the elbow bump and even foot bump have been suggested as substitutes for kisses and handshakes.

尽管如此，时代在变化。有人建议用各种形式的问候语，例如肘部碰撞，甚至脚部碰撞，来代替亲吻和握手。

The International Business Times asked in a large headline: "Will the Asian alternative to handshake make headway now?"

《国际商业时报》曾以醒目标题写道:"亚洲人见面的各种问候方式将会替代现在的握手方式吗?"

The Western handshake can be traced to Greece in the 5th century BC, when it was used as a gesture of peace to show you weren't holding a weapon. It has spread worldwide. But in the 21st century, the need to guard against new viruses may lead to change.

西方的握手可以追溯到公元前 5 世纪的希腊,当时它被用作和平手势,表明你没有拿着武器。握手问候已经遍及全球,但是在进入 21 世纪的今天,防范新病毒的需求可能会导致这种问候方式发生改变。

There are those who favor the Japanese bow. Others prefer the practice common in large parts of southern Asia of holding the palms together, fingers pointing upward in front of the chest, with the head slightly bowed.

有些人赞成日本鞠躬互致问候的方式,也有人喜欢在南亚大部分地区惯用的方法,将手掌放在一起,手指指向胸部前方,头部略微弯曲。

China has several traditional options to offer, including the ancient fist-and-palm salute, which is said to go back 3,000 years. In modern China, it is used on traditional occasions. Traditionally, two people would look at each other during the gesture, raising their hands to their brows and shaking them gently three times.

中国有几种传统问候方式可以选择，包括古时的抱拳礼，据说这种问候礼可以追溯到 3 000 年前。在当代中国，这种礼仪也常用在传统节日等场合。还有一种传统流传下来的打招呼礼仪，就是两个人会互相看着对方，将手举到眉毛的位置，然后轻轻摇动三下。

Foreigners may be more familiar with the hold-fist salute from martial arts movies. In this gesture, the right hand is made into a fist and the left hand is held straight against the fist.

外国人可能会对中国武术电影中的抱拳礼更为熟悉。这种见面礼的姿势是，右手握拳，左手伸直抵住拳头。

Giving up the handshake is a major cultural change, but not preparing could put you in an awkward situation like German Chancellor Angela Merkel. She was recently pictured holding out her hand in greeting only to have her own interior minister decline it. Though the world has appropriated the handshake through the ages, perhaps it's time for a change.

见面放弃握手是一项重大的文化变革，但没有做好准备可能会让您陷入德国总理安吉拉·默克尔这样的尴尬境地：最近一次会晤，她被拍到伸出一只手准备打招呼，结果却被自己的内政部长婉拒与之握手了。虽然长久以来世界各国已经习惯了握手，但现在也许是时候改变了。

Unit 2

Talking about Movies

Warming-up

A. Match the following words with the corresponding pictures:

| movie/film   activities   scene   *soul*   ticket   box office |

1. _____   2. _____   3. _____

4. _____   5. _____   6. _____

B. Use the above words to complete the following sentences:

1. They went abroad for a change of _____.
2. During this month, a lot of _____ will be held.
3. I have 2 _____ for the movie.
4. The film has taken $180 million at the _____.
5. Have you seen the latest _____?
6. Pixar's _____ is a film about a jazz pianist.

Unit 2

 Part 1 Reading Aloud

Task: Read the following passage aloud

Hey, guys! It's Wang Lili here and I'm going to talk about movies with you today.

Now, I should probably start by saying I love winter. I love winter activities like skiing and snowshoeing, and I love the snow. But my favorite thing to do is to curl up on a cozy couch and watch a classic movie or show.

So today, I'm going to talk about some of my favorite winter films and some of the TV shows that I've been watching this season. Most of these take place during the holidays or feature beautiful snowy scenes.

So without further ado, let's take a look at my top 5 picks.

Examine Tips

When reading English, we should pay attention to the following matters and master the relevant skills:

- To take your pronunciation to the next level, focus on stress and intonation.
- Pay attention to the word stress rules.

Part 2   Questions & Answers

Task One

Suppose you are going to see a movie at a movie theater. Read the following poster and you are required to ask 3 questions for detailed information.

Soul

Chinese Name：《心灵奇旅》
English Name: **Soul**
Presents: Disney PIXAR
Director: Peter Docter
Date: Question 1
Ticket Price: Question 2
Time: Question 3

Useful questions:

● Ask the time:

When will the movie begin?
What time will the show start?

● Ask the price:

How much is the picture?
What is the price of the ticket?

Task Two

Based on the same poster for the movie, read the following dialogue between two friends, Wang Lili(W) and Li Lei(L). Suppose you are Wang Lili, while reading, you are required to complete the conversation by answering Li Lei's questions.

Soul

Chinese Name: 《心灵奇旅》
English Name: *Soul*
Presents: Disney PIXAR
Director: Peter Docter
Date：December 25, 2020
Ticket Price: $15 for 3D
Time: 7:00PM

W: Li Lei, would you like to see a movie tonight?

L: Sure. Which movie do you have in mind?

W: There are so many winter blockbusters. They all look good! I'm so excited to see this IMAX movie Soul!

L: Okay. Did you buy the tickets? Can you check the price?

W: _____.

L: Sounds good. When does it start?

W: _____.

L: Got it. How about we meet at the theater at 6:30? I want to get some popcorn before the show.

W: Yeah. But we still have to choose our seats.

L: Ok, where should we sit?

W: I don't want to sit in the front. It's too close to the screen.

L: Ok. Are there any empty seats in the middle?

W: Let me see. No, there aren't. They're all taken.

L: Oh, too bad! This movie is really popular. Let's sit in the back.

W: Sounds good. I see two seats next to each other!

L: Perfect!

Examine Tips

- When answering a question, pay attention to the special interrogative pronoun or special interrogative adverb of the question, find the corresponding text content in the notice, and make a correct answer;
- The expression of information such as date, time and price.

Part 3 Chinese-English Interpretation

Task: In this part, you are required to translate a short speech into English orally.

Joe: 音乐是我朝思暮想的全部,是我活着的理由。我只是害怕如果我今天死去,我的生命会毫无意义。

Libba: 我听过一条小鱼的故事。它游到一条大鱼旁边说,"我想找到名叫大海的东西。""大海?"大鱼问,"你现在就在大海里啊。""这儿吗?"小鱼说,"这里只有水啊,我想要的是大海。"所以,现在你觉得自己会做些什么呢?你会怎样过完一生?

Joe: 我不确定,但我知道,我会享受生命的每一分钟。

——***Soul***《心灵奇旅》

Useful sentences for the story:

- It's my reason for living.
- I heard this story about a fish.
- That's what you're in right now.
- What I want is the ocean.
- I'm going to live every minute of it.

Part 4　Presentation

Task: In this part, you are required to talk about what is shown in the following diagrams, describing and summarizing its contents. You should add your own comments.

Survey about the 2019 and 2018 Box Office during National Day Holiday.

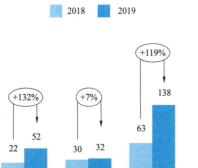

2019 vs. 2018 Box Office Performance of Films During National Day Holiday group^m

*National Day Holiday: 30th Sep-8th Oct.

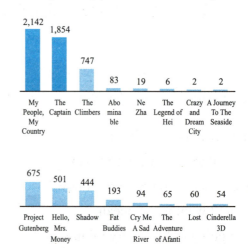

2019 vs. 2018 TOP8 Films During National Day Holiday (Box Office: ten million)

*The films ranked according to total box office

Useful sentences patterns:

● At the beginning:

1. It can be seen from the statistics that...
2. The chart gives information that...

- while describing:

1. There was a rise/increase/upward trend from...to...
2. It has risen to an average of...

- At the end:

1. The graph reflects that...
2. From the data we gathered from the above graph, we can conclude that...
3. According to what has been discussed above, we can arrive at the conclusion that...

Words List

1. skiing [skiːɪŋ]   n.   滑雪运动
2. snowshoeing ['snəʊˌʃuːɪŋ]   n.   穿雪鞋行走
3. favorite ['feɪvərɪt, 'feɪvrɪt]   adj.   最受喜爱的
4. curl [kɜːl]   v.   卷曲；盘绕
5. cozy ['kəʊzi]   adj.   舒适的；友好的；密切的
6. couch [kaʊtʃ]   n.   床；长沙发；卧榻
7. classic ['klæsɪk]   adj.   经典的；古典的；最优秀的
8. snowy ['snəʊɪ]   adj.   下雪的；被雪覆盖的；洁白无瑕的
9. director [dɪ'rɛktə, daɪ-]   n.   导演；主任；主管
10. performance [pə'fɔːməns]   n.   表现；绩效；表演

Practice after the unit

Exercise 1   Ask questions about the underlined parts:

1. The movie starts at 8 o'clock.

2. Tickets are $30 for 3D.

3. I often see a movie in the evening.

4. Tom saw a movie at a theater yesterday.

5. I will go to the movies tomorrow morning.

6. Paul likes to go to the movies.

Exercise 2   Translate the following sentences into English:

1. 这是我努力学习的理由。

2. 我听说过关于心灵的一个故事。

3. 我想要的是幸福。我会享受生命的每一分钟。

4. 这幅图表对比了 2018 年和 2019 年的国庆假期票房情况。

5. 正如以上柱状图中所看到的，2019 年的国庆票房取得了巨大成功。

6. 从以上分析，我们可以得出结论，制作精良的正能量中国电影将会得到青睐。

Unit 2

Reference answers

Part 2

Task One

Question 1: When will the film be released?
Question 2: What is the price of the ticket?
Question 3: What time does the movie start?

Task Two

Tickets are $15 for 3D.
It starts at 7.

Part 3

Joe: Music is all I think about from the moment I wake up in the morning to the moment I fell asleep at night. It's my reason for living. I'm just afraid that if I died today that my life would've amounted to nothing.

Libba: I heard this story about a fish. He swims up to this older fish and says, "I'm trying to find this thing they call the ocean." "The ocean?" says the older fish, "That's what you're in right now." "This?" says the young fish, "This is water. What I want is the ocean." So what do you think you'll do? How are you gonna spend your life?

Joe: I'm not sure. But I do know… I'm going to live every minute of it.

——*Soul*

Part 4

As can be seen from the graph, the films in 2019 National Day achieved great success with an increase of 100%+ YOY in the total box office. The films ranking showed cliff feature and central themed pieces emerged as the best.

The films in 2019 National Day achieved great success with an increase of 132% YOY in total box office and 119% YOY in the number of audience. The total box office of films released in 2019 National Day Holiday reached RMB 52 bn.

Compared with films released in 2018 National Day Holiday, the films ranking owned cliff feature while central themed pieces emerged as the best. Among them, "My People, My Country" and "The Captain" gained an outstanding performance.

The important events and anniversaries could stimulate the audience's enthusiasm. These three movies made a good beginning. Meanwhile, the most satisfied factor of the three movies is "Positive Energy".

According to the information gathered above, we may reach the conclusion that with the audience's increasing appreciation and taste, the acting, appearance and special effect are no longer the regular assessment. The movies which have Chinese Mood with excellent production mode are more appreciated.

Unit 2

Bilingual Reading Time

Jobs that keep film sets running
电影中的那些幕后工作

It's not only real actors who need costume designers, but animated characters as well. At Pixar, there are people who are specifically hired to animate clothing, like tailoring and simulation artist Kris Campbell.

不仅真实的演员需要服装设计师，动画角色也需要服装设计师。在皮克斯动画工作室，有些人专门被雇来制作服装动画，比如裁剪和模拟艺术家 Kris Campbell。

They have to design and model clothes and then make sure they fit on the animated characters. This process involves computer simulations to make sure the fabric moves correctly.

他们设计并模拟服装，确保服装适合动画角色。他们还要在电脑上进行模拟，以确保布料移动的方向是正确的。

In "Coco," for example, these simulations helped them prevent clothes from getting stuck in the skeleton characters 'bones.

例如，在《寻梦环游记》中，这些模拟动画帮助他们防止衣服卡在骷髅角色的骨骼上。

Productions try to use real food whenever they can, and when they do, a food stylist comes to handle it all. It's a lot more than just altering dishes to fit an actor's dietary restrictions, though that is certainly part of the job.

制片公司会尽量使用真实的食物，当他们需要使用真实的食物时，会由食物设计师来制作。食物设计师不仅仅是改变食物以适应演员的饮食限制，当然，这也是工作的一部分。

Food stylist Zoe Hegedus had to solve a number of different problems on the set of "Midsommar."

在拍摄《仲夏夜惊魂》时，食品设计师 Zoe Hegedus 必须解决许多不同的问题。

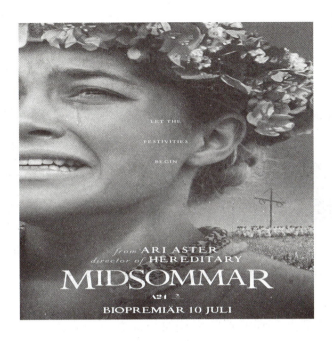

The film was mostly shot outdoors in the heat, so she had to make sure the food both looked and stayed fresh.

影片大多是在高温下拍摄的,所以她必须确保食物既美观又新鲜。

Sometimes, this was as easy as spraying a potato with cooking spray to make it look like it just came out of the oven.

有时候很简单,比如在土豆上喷洒烹饪喷雾剂,看起来就像刚从烤箱里拿出来一样。

Other dishes needed to be altered entirely to beat the heat.

而有些食物则需要进行彻底的改变,以防止食物在高温下变质。

  For example, those meat pies you see on screen are't filled with real meat, which would spoil quickly. Instead, Hegedus cooked oatmeal and colored it brown, giving it the look and texture of chopped meat.

  例如，你在屏幕上看到的那些肉馅饼里面并不是真肉，真肉会很快变质的。Hegedus 将燕麦片煮熟并涂成棕色，让它的外观和质地看起来像碎肉。

Unit 3

Seeing a Doctor

Warming-up

A. Match the following words with the corresponding pictures:

| temperature   fever   medicine   injection   psychologist   clinic |

1. _____
2. _____
3. _____

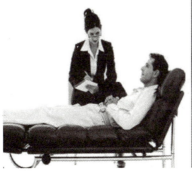

4. _____
5. _____
6. _____

B. Use the above words to complete the following sentences:

1. Charles was at the _____ recovering from an operation on his arm.
2. The doctor has given me some _____ to take for my cough.
3. Your forehead is burning. Have you got a _____?
4. When you have been feeling stressed for a while, you'd better make an appointment with the _____.
5. The nurse pressed the patient a bit too hard when she gave him an _____.
6. Painkillers are very useful in small amounts to bring your _____ down.

Unit 3

Part 1 Reading Aloud

  Li Lei was ill yesterday so that he went to see a doctor. A nurse took his temperature after he got to the waiting room. Then he went to the doctor's room, there the doctor looked him over and said he had a bad cold with a fever. In another room the nurse gave him an injection, after that he went home with some medicine. But he felt even worse when he saw the bill of treatment cost. Then he thought of a news read on the internet months ago that a patient spent five million and five hundred thousand dollars during his 66 days' treatment in hospital. Moreover, the reports about the high profit of the medicine are getting more and more. It is too expensive for most of people to see a doctor. Therefore, people are all complaining about the high cost of the treatment. So just like Li Lei, we all hope the government can carry out some measures to control this situation to give people a satisfactory medical service environment.

Tips for reading: Intonation

I. Falling tone

A. Statements：
  He works hard every day. ↘
  I'm Amy from Shanghai. ↘

B. Special questions：
  How do you go to school? ↘
  When will you come? ↘

C. Exclamations：
  How clever she is! ↘
  What a great museum! ↘

II. Rising tone

A. General questions:

　　Are you a doctor?↗

　　Would you like some soup?↗

B. Declarative questions:

　　You are a policeman?↗

　　He lives here?↗

G. Asking for repetition:

　　Pardon?↗　　What?↗　　Who?↗　　When?↗　　For what?↗

Unit 3

Part 2 Questions & Answers

Task One

Suppose you are Li Lei, you feel much mental stress and you are calling to make an appointment with a psychologist. Read the following poster and you are required to ask 3 questions for detailed information.

> Psychologist Clinic Schedule of KS No.1 Hospital
>
> Psychologist: David Smith
> Speciality: <u>Question 1</u>
> Schedule: <u>Question 2</u>
> Place: Room 305 Building No. 2
> Contact Person: Lily Wang
> Telephone Number: <u>Question 3</u>
> Internet Website: www.ksrmyy.org

Useful sentences for questions:

A. Asking for a doctor's speciality:
   What is his speciality?
   What does he specialize in?
   What is he good /excellent at?
   What is he skilled in?
   What is his major?
   What does he major in?
B. Asking for a doctor's schedule:
   What is the psychologist's schedule?
   When can I see the psychologist?

When will the psychologist be in the outpatient service?

C. Asking for the contact information:

How can I contact the psychologist?

What is the telephone number?

Can you tell me the telephone number?

What is the website of the hospital?

Task Two

Suppose you are Psychologist Smith who are talking with the patient Li Lei about mental stress, complete the conversation by answering Li Lei's questions based on the following poster.

Psychologist Clinic Schedule of KS No.1 Hospital

Psychologist: David Smith
Speciality: mental stress
Schedule: Monday (8:00am–4:30pm), Wednesday morning (8:00am–11:30am)
Place: Room 305 Building No. 2
Contact Person: Lily Wang
Telephone Number: 0512-57559009
Internet Website: www.ksrmyy.org

About Mental Stress:
People Involved: white-collar employees, brain-workers
Main Reasons: increasing competition, too much stress
Main Symptoms: weak, forgetful, ill-tempered
Suggestions: regulating moods, making friends, traveling

David Smith: Good morning, what can I do for you?
Li Lei: Good morning. I have been feeling down recently, weak, forgetful and ill-tempered.
David Smith: You've got too much mental stress, I think.

Li Lei: Yes, I am. I'm always stressed.
David Smith: Don't worry. Many people feel stressed.
Li Lei: Usually what kind of people feel stressed?
David Smith: _____.
Li Lei: Why?
David Smith: _____.
Li Lei: Then how can I cope with the mental stress?
David Smith: _____.
Li Lei: Thank you, I'll have a try.

Part 3 Chinese-English Interpretation

> Task: In this part, you are required to translate the following dialogue between Lily and his doctor into English orally.

医生在诊室里给病人莉莉看病：

莉莉：您好，医生！

医生：您好，您需要什么帮助？

莉莉：医生，我感觉不太舒服。

医生：能描述一下您的感觉吗？

莉莉：我咳嗽差不多一周了，吃了药但没起作用，所以来您这里问一下我的病。

医生：您头疼吗？

莉莉：最近经常头疼，有时候爬完楼梯后我会感到很虚弱，甚至要晕倒。

医生：不要担心，我想您只是感冒了，还有就是您让自己太累了。稍等一下，我给您开一个治疗意见，记住按要求吃药，好好休息，很快就会好起来的。

莉莉：谢谢您，医生。

Useful sentences for seeing a doctor:

A. Doctors:

How do you feel now?

What's your trouble?

What's wrong with you?

What seems to be bothering you?

How long have you been like this?

I will have to give you an injection.

I want to say you've caught a heavy cold.

Take this medicine two times a day.

B. Patients:

    I feel terrible.

    I don't feel very well.

    I've got a headache.

    I feel very tired and weak.

    I don't want to take the medicine.

    Do I need to be hospitalized?

    Can I go back to work tomorrow?

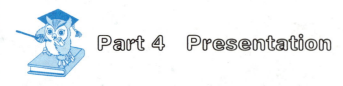

Part 4 Presentation

Task: In this part, you are required to talk about what is shown in the following diagram, describing and summarizing its contents. You should add your own comments.

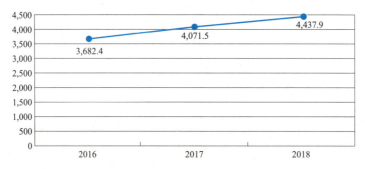

The number of mental patients (10 thousand)

Useful sentences for describing graphs:

A. Describing the increasing or decreasing

  1) The number of ... grew/rose/increased(decreased/declined/dropped/fell) from... to...

  2) There was a big/huge/dramatic/sharp/sudden/gradual/steady increase (decrease) in...

B. Describing the peak or bottom

  1) ... reached a peak of / peaked at ... in the year of...

  2) ... amounted to ... in ...

  3) ... reached the bottom of ...in ....

C. Describing the time
- 1) in/around/before/after/since 1985
- 2) from 1985 to 1986; over the period from 1985 to 1986
- 3) by the next decade
- 4) in the second quarter of this year
- 5) in/during the 1980's
- 6) during the past half century

Words List

1. treatment ['tri:tmənt]   n.   治疗；诊治；疗法；对待
2. speciality [ˌspeʃi'æləti]   n.   专业；专长
3. schedule ['ʃedju:l]   n.   日程安排；工作计划
4. outpatient ['aʊtpeɪʃnt]   n.   门诊病人；门诊部
5. stress [stres]   n.   精神压力；心理负担；紧张；压力
6. forgetful [fə'getfl]   adj.   健忘的；疏忽的
7. ill-tempered [ˌɪl'tempəd]   adj.   脾气暴躁的；动辄发怒的
8. hospitalize ['hɒspɪtəlaɪz]   v.   送（某人）入院治疗
9. symptom ['sɪmptəm]   n.   症状；征候
10. regulate ['regjuleɪt]   v.   （用规则条例）约束；控制；管理；调节

Unit 3

Practice after the unit

Exercise 1   Ask questions about the underlined parts:

1. Mr. Brown is a dentist.

2. He works in the dentist clinic in Kunshan People's Hospital.

3. He is in the outpatient service on Tuesday (8:00am–4:30pm) and Friday morning (8:00am–11:30am)

4. You can make an appointment with Mr. Brown by calling 0512-57559009 .

5. I have been feeling headache for two days.

6. Take two tablets three times a day after meals.

Exercise 2   Translate the following sentences into English:

1. 早上好，先生，哪里不舒服吗？

2. 我最近感觉情绪低落，健忘，爱发脾气。

3. 我头疼，还咳嗽。

4. 让我给你量一下体温吧。

5. 不要担心，你就是感冒了。

6. 按时吃药，多喝水多休息，你很快就会好的。

Unit 3

Reference answers

Part 2

Task One:

Suppose you are Li Lei, you feel much mental stress and you are calling to make an appointment with a psychologist. Read the following poster and you are required to ask 3 questions for detailed information.
Question 1: What does he specialize in?
Question 2: When can I see the psychologist?
Question 3: How can I contact the psychologist?

Task Two:

Suppose you are Psychologist Smith who are talking with the patient Li Lei about mental stress, complete the conversation by answering Li Lei's questions based on the following poster.

David Smith: Good morning, what can I do for you?
Li Lei: Good morning. I have been feeling down recently, weak, forgetful and ill-tempered.
David Smith: You've got too much mental stress, I think.
Li Lei: Yes, I am. I'm always stressed.
David Smith: Don't worry. Many people feel stressed.
Li Lei: Usually what kind of people feel stressed?
David Smith: White-collars and brain-workers often get stressed.
Li Lei: Why?
David Smith: There are too many competitions for work, so many of them feel too much mental stress with the increasing competitions.
Li Lei: Then how can I cope with the mental stress?
David Smith: First of all, try to relax yourself and regulate your moods. Secondly, making some friends will be helpful, you can share your feelings with

them. Lastly, try to find some time to travel, traveling is a best way to relax, beautiful scenery can release your mental stress.

Li Lei: Thank you, I'll have a try.

Part 3

The doctor is asking about the illness of his patient Lily in his clinic.

Lily: Hello, doctor.

Doctor: Hello, what can I do for you?

Lily: I don't feel well, doctor.

Doctor: Can you describe how you feel?

Lily: I have coughed for almost a week. I took some medicine, but it didn't work. So I come here to ask about my illness.

Doctor: Do you have headaches?

Lily: I had headaches quite often these days, and sometimes I even got faint after climbing stairs.

Doctor: Don't worry. I think you have caught a cold and also you have made yourself too tired. Wait a moment, I'll give you some suggestions. Remember to take medicines as required and have a good rest, you will be fine soon.

Lily: Thank you, doctor.

Part 4

The graph offers us the information about the number of mental patients from 2016 to 2018. As the graph shows above, the number of mental patients experienced a gradual rise from 36,824 thousand to 44,379 thousand.

Why did the number of mental patients keep rising significantly? I think the main reason is the increasing competition in the society which caused people too much stress. As far as adults are concerned, most of them support a family, they have to care for the elderly and bring up children, and maybe they have to pay for the house loan and car mortgage, so they have to work harder and harder, but there are too much challenge including their work and new comers. Therefore they have too much stress both at home and at work. If they cannot release the stress in time, the stress may cause them some mental illness.

Then how to help people relieve the pressure and decrease the number of mental patients? In my opinion, mental illness is nothing to be ashamed of. If we feel something wrong, we should go to see a psychologist to get treatment at once. Meanwhile, we are supposed to learn to regulate ourselves' moods, smile to the life, work hard and work smiled. In daily life, try to make more friends, talk with them and play with them, which can make us feel good no matter whether they offer help or not. In addition, we can go for a travel. Traveling in a strange place can easily make us forget work and pressure. Enjoying the beautiful scenery in a new place is a good way to release stress and to help treat mental illness.

Bilingual Reading Time

Traditional Chinese medicine in foreigners' eyes
外国人眼中的中医

Have you had any experience with traditional Chinese medicine? Do you think it is effective? Some people share their opinions of TCM and also some experiences. Please feel free to join in!

你看过中医吗？你觉得效果如何？下面是来自世界各地的一些人对于中医的看法和经历。你的看法是什么？

Motika (Swede)

Nothing wrong with TCM, East Europe still has herbal pharmacies in use. That is recommended first-then "chemicals" (Western medicine) as a last resort.

我觉得中医挺好的，东欧人也喜欢中草药，一般生了病都是先考虑能不能吃中草药，不行的话再吃西药。

Aziz (Bangladeshi)

I have had great experiences with Chinese herbal medicine and acupuncture. My baby daughter was cured by a herbal liquid made by the hospital for a cough which was about to turn into bronchitis. A US-educated doctor failed to help her with a Western type of injection and medicine. Then the doctor suggested local traditional medicine and after the sixth day of TCM treatment, all the symptoms had disappeared. But it must be said that anybody would vomit when tasting the liquid that we had to give to an 8-month-old girl. There are many kinds of herbs, but make sure you are taking advice from a proper doctor, and it is better to collect the medicine from the hospital, as there are lots of fake medicines nowadays.

我对中草药和针灸印象相当好。我的小女儿有一次咳嗽得厉害，都快变成支气管炎了，后来喝中药治好了。一个从美国留学回来的大夫用西医的疗法给她治病，一点用也没有。后来他建议我们去看中医，结果治了6天病就好了。但是那药真是难喝啊，谁要是喝一口非得吐了不可，而我们却得让8个月大的女儿喝这个。中草药有很多种，你一定要去看一位靠谱的大夫，而且最好在医院抓药，因为现在市面上的假药太多了。

Seanboyce (British)

I have read a lot of studies about the ineffectiveness of many Chinese treatments. The few miracle cases can be put down to statistical anomalies or placebo effect which has been proven to be better than quack medicine in some cases. Chinese medicine really does fail when it comes under the scrutiny of scientific method... Maybe it does work, but I personally don't believe in it.

我读过很多关于中国疗法无效的研究。为数不多的奇迹病例可以归结为统计异常或安慰剂效应，这已被证明在某些情况下优于庸医。在科学方法的监督下，中医确实失败了……也许它确实有用，但我个人并不相信它。

Laowai (British)

My wife is a TCM practitioner so that is always the first port of call. However, she does accept that in some cases Western medicine is more effective. Whether you choose Chinese or Western medicine, it can be difficult to know if either was successful as the problem might have cleared up without any connection to the treatment. There is also the placebo effect to consider.

我老婆就是一名中医，所以生了病肯定首选中药。但她也承认在一些情况下还是西药比较有效。不过无论你选择中医还是西医，都很难说哪种更有效，因为很多症状就算你不管它它也会好，况且吃药本身也有安慰作用。

Sdivester (American)

TCM is difficult but not impossible to find in the US. However, if you go to your local GNC, many supplements on sale contain Chinese herbs or medicine. Many Western medicines are derived from plant-based materials, so TCM does have its place in society.

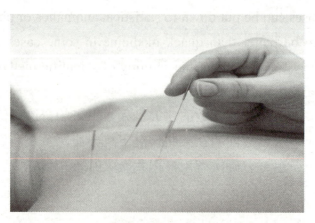

中药在美国并不多见但还是有的。如果你去当地的保健品商店，你会看见货架上摆着许多中药。况且很多西药其实也是从草本植物里提炼出来的，所以说中药还是有市场的。

Seneca (American)

Chinese medicine regards the human body as a system that needs constant fine-tuning and medico-chemical measures, so as to avoid contracting diseases, whereas Western medicine treats the human body after the illness or disease starts manifesting itself. As I see it, Chinese people are more likely to take Chinese traditional medicine, herbal teas and observe "cold" or "hot" warnings for food than Westerners. Westerners drink icy-cold drinks in hot weather too often, and this can lead to conditions such as a hoarse voice, inflamed throat, colds, upset stomach, diarrhea.

中医把人体看成一个系统，而且需要不断调理，避免生病。而西医则注重得病以后该怎样治疗。据我观察，中国人似乎更喜欢中医，更喜欢花草茶，更重视食物的是凉是热。西方人在天气热的时候特别喜欢喝冷饮，像这样毫无节制地喝冷饮对声带不好，容易导致嗓子发炎、感冒、胃病还有腹泻。

Ghost Buster (American)

Traditional Chinese Medicine needs a more scientific approach. No kind of medicine is a cure for everything. If we could find a way to combine all knowledge of both Eastern and Western medicine, then we could perhaps find a way to cure all diseases. The major difference between Traditional Chinese Medicine and Western

Medicine is that the former treats an illness or sickness as a component of the entire body's system, while the latter treats it as a single isolated component. Each condition or disease is best treated by one of these types of medicine. In other words, no single medicine is superior to the other.

中医需要更科学的治疗方法，无论是中医还是西医，谁都不能包治百病。如果我们能够将中西方的智慧结合在一起，说不定就能把所有的病都治好了呢。中西医最大的不同是，中医在治病的时候着眼于全身，而西医则专注于局部。不同疾病最佳的治疗方式不同，换句话说，无论是中医还是西医，没有谁比谁更好一说。

（Taken from CRI NEWS Plus 英语环球广播）

Unit 4

Having an Interview

Warming-up

A. Match the following words with the corresponding pictures:

| reception   secretary   interview   table   leisure   poster |

1. _____

2. _____

3. _____

4. _____

5. _____

6. _____

B. Use the above words to complete the following sentences:

1. At the beginning of the conference, all the visitors are required to report at the _____.
2. He talked about the amusing story of his _____ in his first job.
3. There is a _____ of contents at the front of this dictionary.
4. They put up _____ all round the town advertising the circus.
5. My mother is very busy; she rarely get much _____ time.
6. Mary got a job as personal _____ to the company CEO.

Unit 4

Part 1 Reading Aloud

Task: Read the following passage aloud

Holiday Inn is a world-renowned hotel, founded in 1952 in the United States. The hotel includes medium-high and mid-grade hotels with moderate prices and elegant environment. After years of hard work, Holiday Inn is now developing rapidly in China, with its business in Shanghai, Beijing, Suzhou and other major cities. It is a perfect place both for business and leisure travelers with an international style of design, relaxed environment and a comfortable, pleasant atmosphere. Holiday Inn is committed to providing every guest with care at every moment, adhering to the principle and concept of "DO WHATEVER YOU WANT, LEAVE THE REST TO US."

Examine Tips

When expressing themselves, people usually pause in a sense group in order to make them understood clearly. The following points indicate where you should have a pause:
- Before a noun phrase;
- After a noun phrase, prepositional phrase, non-predicative phrase;
- Before or after all kinds of clauses.
- A phrase can not be separated in meaning or grammar.

Part 2 Questions & Answers

Task One

Suppose you are an INTERVIEWEE. Read the following poster and you are required to ask 3 questions for detailed information.

Wanted

We need you

Position: <u>Question 1</u>
Workplace：Suzhou City
Interview Time: <u>Question 2</u>
Requirements: <u>Question 3</u>
ADD: No. 12 Renmin Road, Gusu District Suzhou City
TEL(FAX): 0517-6668889
Contact person: Mr. Chen

Task Two

Based on the same poster, read the following dialogue. Suppose you are Wang Lili, while reading, you are required to complete the conversation by answering Li Lei's questions.

Unit 4

Wanted

We need you

Position: Receptionist (We need two)

Workplace：Suzhou City

Interview Time: May 12 to May 18, 2021

Requirements: Female (preferred age 20 to 28), excellent proficiency in English, good team player.

ADD: No. 12 Renmin Road, Gusu District Suzhou City

TEL(FAX): 0517-6668889

Contact person: Mr. Chen

L: Hi Wang Lili. How's everything going?.

W: Hi Li Lei. Good to see you. I've just read the poster of Holiday Inn. The hotel wants two receptionists and I am quite interested in it.

L: That's great! I heard Holiday Inn is a five-star hotel. Where is it?

W: _____.

L: That's not far from our school. And what's the requirements?

W: _____.

L: Oh. It sounds so strict. But I'm sure you can get the job.

W: Thank you. Hope I can pass the interview successfully.

L: You get to show a better one of yourself. Good luck to you!

W: Thank you so much and bye.

L: Bye-bye.

Examine Tips

- Pay attention to the expression of the date. The order should be Day-Month-Year or Month-Day-Year.
- The date should be pronounced in English not in Chinese.
- The order for the address should be arranged from small to large. It could not be reversed in English.

Part 3 Chinese-English Interpretation

Task: In this part, you are required to translate a short speech into English orally.

我从广告上得知贵公司需要秘书故来申请。我叫李磊,23岁,在硅湖学院学习经济管理,今年夏天即将毕业。我精通计算机操作及办公软件的使用,这能够帮助我做好办公室工作。另外,我十分喜欢办公室工作,并且我也认为我能胜任这个工作。如果我能有机会得到这份工作,我会十分感激。盼望收到您的回信。

Useful sentences for an interview:

- I learned from your advertisement that your company is in need of an engineer.
- I am proficient in /good at /have a good command of the computer science.
- I will appreciate it very much if you give me the opportunity.
- Thank you for your consideration. I am looking forward to receiving your reply.

Unit 4

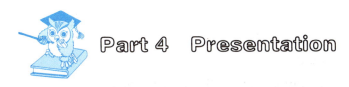 Part 4 Presentation

Task: In this part, you are required to talk about what is shown in the following diagram, describing and summarizing its contents. You should add your own comments.

A survey on the average income from different educational backgrounds

Average income in each year ($) / Education degree	2017	2018	2019	2020
Master's degree or above	30,000	32,000	36,000	40,000
Bachelor's degree	10,000	13,000	18,000	20,000
Vocational college	6,660	8,330	8,350	10,000
High school	5,000	5,200	5,350	5,430
Less than high school	3,310	3,500	3,650	3,780

Useful sentences patterns:

- At the beginning:

1. The graph/chart/table above shows / describes / illustrates that.....
2. From the above graph/chart, it can be seen that…

3. The chart/table shows the differences between…

● while describing:

1. There was a great /slight increase /rise in…
2. The number /rate has nearly doubled, compared with that of last year.
3. The number is…times as much as that of….

● At the end:

1. It's clear/evident from the chart that… / We can draw the conclusion that…
2. From what has been discussed above/Taking into account all these factors, we can draw the conclusion that…
3. There is no doubt that special attention must be paid to the problem of…
4. It is high time that we put an end to the tendency of…

Words List

1. reception [rɪˈsepʃn]		n.	接待处，接待区
2. moderate [ˈmɒdərət, ˈmɒdəreɪt]		adj.	适度的，中等的，温和的
3. elegant [ˈelɪgənt]		adj.	优雅的，精美的
4. major [ˈmeɪdʒə(r)]		adj.	主要的，重要的，大的
5. leisure [ˈleʒə(r)]		n.	休闲，空闲，闲暇
6. relaxed [rɪˈlækst]		adj.	放松的，自在的
7. atmosphere [ˈætməsfɪə(r)]		n.	大气，气氛，氛围
8. be committed to			投入，致力于，旨在
9. adhere to			坚持，遵守
10. principle [ˈprɪnsəpl]		n.	原则，原理
11. concept [ˈkɒnsept]		n.	概念，理念
12. poster [ˈpəʊstə(r)]		n.	海报
13. receptionist [rɪˈsepʃənɪst]		n.	接待员
14. proficiency [prəˈfɪʃnsi]		n.	熟练，精通
15. secretary [ˈsekrətri]		n.	秘书
16. table [ˈteɪbl]		n.	表，表格

Practice after the unit

Exercise 1   Match the two columns together:

1. How often do you check your e-mails every week?
2. What do yo usually do in your spare time?
3. Which kind of music do you prefer, pop or classical?
4. When were you born?
5. Where have you been these days?
6. Who can I contact if there is any problem?

a. I've been to Chongqing, my hometown.
b. Every two days.
c. Riding bicycles with my friends.
d. On June 2nd, 2005.
e. Please contact our manager, Ms. Wu.
f. Classical music is my favorite.

Exercise 2   Translate the following sentences into English:

1. 我从报纸上得知贵公司正在招聘秘书。
2. 如果我能有机会获得这份工作，我将不胜感激。
3. 上面这张表格清楚地向我们展示了酒店第一季度的利润情况。
4. 和去年相比，这一数字成倍增加了。
5. 毫无疑问这些现象都具有共同的原因。

Unit 4

Reference answers

Warming-up

A.
1. interview   2. leisure   3. reception
4. secretary   5. poster   6. table

B.
1. reception   2. interview   3. table
4. posters   5. leisure   6. secretary

Part 2

Task One

　　Question 1. What is the position?
　　Question 2. When will the interview take place?
　　Question 3. What are the requirements?

Task Two

　　It is in Suzhou City.
　　Female (preferred age 20 to 28), excellent proficiency in English, good team player.

Part 3

　　I have learned from an advertisement that your company is in need of a secretary and I would like to apply for the position. My name is Li Lei and I'm 20 years old. I am studying business management in Silicon Lake College and I will graduate this summer. I am proficient in computer operation and office software, which can help me do the office work very well. And I have learned English for ten years. What's more, I enjoy office work very much and I believe I am qualified for the job. I will appreciate it very much if you would give me the opportunity. Looking forward to your reply.

Part 4

The above table clearly shows us that different education gets different pays. We see that one with higher education background earns more money yearly than those with lower ones. For instance, the vocational college students get paid $10,000 every year whereas those with a Bachelor's degree can earn $20,000 in 2020.

Several reasons, in my opinion, can be identified to account for this phenomenon. To begin with, compared with those with comparatively lower education degree, people who have received higher education possess considerably wider knowledge, more remarkable learning and research ability, greater innovation and most of all, resourceful social network, all of which are essential to a high-income work. Also, the higher one's education degree is, the bigger platform he will have to show his ability. For example, his college, university, or research institute will organize various job fairs for them to communicate face to face with employers.

This phenomenon tells us that education is a worthy investment. Therefore, substantial education investment should be strengthened while we, as college students, should study harder to build our country and strive for a better life for ourselves.

Unit 4

Bilingual Reading Time

Chinese college graduates' job seeking choices more diversified: survey
调查显示：中国大学生择业选择越来越多样化

China's fresh college graduates have shown interest in a wider range of occupations during the ongoing spring recruitment season, according to a survey recently conducted by China Youth Daily.

据《中国青年报》最近进行的一项调查显示，在正在进行的春季招聘季中，我国应届大学毕业生表现出了对多种职业的兴趣。

The survey of 1,690 new graduates showed that jobs with more stability or more flexibility as well as ones in emerging industries are all favored by the students.

这项针对 1 690 名应届毕业生的调查显示，学生们更青睐那些更稳定、更灵活的工作，以及新兴行业的工作。

Specifically, 61 percent of those surveyed would like to have a relatively stable job such as a teacher or civil servant, 49 percent may also pursue a career with more flexibility such as the internet or real estate industry, and 41 percent would work in new emerging industries such as live streaming.

具体来说，61%的受访者希望有一个相对稳定的工作，如教师或公务员；49%受访者希望从事互联网或房地产等更灵活的行业；41%受访者希望从事直播等新兴行业。

In the survey, 65.3 percent of those interviewed said a majority of the graduates-to-be they know have received job offers.

调查显示，65.3%的受访者表示，他们认识的大多数大学毕业生都已获得了工作机会。

It also found that 37.8 percent of students have no plans to work in crowded major cities, and 30.9 percent of those surveyed are inclined to start their career from the grassroots level.

调查还发现，37.8%的受访者没有在一线大城市工作的计划，30.9%的受访者倾向于从基层开始职业生涯。

In 2020, demand for recruitment by Chinese enterprises increased 26 percent from 2019, compared with a drop of 35 percent globally, according to LinkedIn data and surveys of about 5,500 global human resources managers.

根据领英对全球约 5 500 名人力资源经理的调查和数据显示，2020 年，中国企业对招聘的需求较 2019 年增加了 26%，而全球则下降了 35%。

The employment situation for China's new college graduates has been progressing smoothly this year thanks to joint efforts by central and local governments and universities, the Ministry of Education said. China is expected to see a record 9.09 million college graduates this year, 350,000 more than last year.

教育部表示，在中央和地方政府及高校的共同努力下，今年中国高校毕业生就业形势进展稳畅。中国大学毕业生人数今年预期将达 909 万，相比去年增加 35 万，创下历史新高。

Wang Hui, director of the ministry's department of college student affairs, said although the stable economic recovery in the first quarter has laid a solid foundation for sound employment, the COVID-19 epidemic still has an impact on college students' employment and the situation remains complex and challenging. Since last autumn, the ministry has worked with other departments to launch a campaign to help graduating students find jobs or start businesses.

教育部高校学生司司长王辉表示，今年一季度以来国民经济呈持续稳定恢复态势，为稳定就业奠定了坚实基础，但疫情对大学生就业的影响仍在持续，就业形势依然复杂严峻。自去年秋季以来，教育部已同其他部门发起了一项活动，来帮助毕业生求职或创业。

The ministry launched a 24-hour online campus recruitment service last year to help graduates find jobs amid the epidemic and the service has provided 14.5 million job postings this year, with graduates submitting resumes 37.6 million times.

教育部去年启动了一项 24 小时全天候网上校园招聘服务，帮助毕业生在疫情期间求职，今年这项服务已经提供了 1 405 万个招聘公告，毕业生简历投递达 3 760 万次。

Liu Yuguang, director of China Higher Education Student Information and Career Center, said a recruitment promotion week will be held nationwide from May 17 to 23 to provide both job opportunities for the new graduates and chances for universities and employers to better match candidates with open positions. Each provincial-level region will organize at least two large-scale job fairs during the week。

全国高等学校学生信息咨询与就业指导中心主任刘玉光表示，从 5 月 17 日至 23 日，将在全国范围内举办高校毕业生就业促进周活动，为应届毕业生提供工作机会，也为高校和招聘方提供机会来更好地实现应聘者与空缺岗位的对接。在促进周期间，每个省级地区都会组织至少两次大规模招聘会。

(Extracted from *China Daily*, 2021)

Unit 5

Making a Reservation

Warming-up

> A. Match the following words with the corresponding pictures:

baggage claim area	check-in	information desk
security check	registration form	departure lounge

_____

_____

_____

_____

_____

_____

B. Use the above words to complete the following sentences:

1. Please get familiar with the emergency exit and the position of fire-fighting equipment when you _____ the hotel.
2. They were delayed for 5 hours at the _____ because of the heavy storm.
3. Would you fill in this _____?
4. Please hurry up to pass _____, now it's boarding.
5. The _____ are crowed with people waiting for their luggage to arrive.
6. If you'd like further information on this, there's a guidebook in several languages at _____.

Unit 5

Part 1 Reading Aloud

We're committed to creating a safe and relaxing experience, including delivering an even cleaner stay from check-in to check-out. We encourage guests to use digital check-in and key for a Contactless Arrival experience. With the Hilton Honors app, you can check-in, choose your room, access your room with a Digital Key and check-out using your phone! This option is available at over 4,800 Hilton properties mainly in the US, the UK, and Canada, with availability in other countries where local regulations allow. For those guests who do not have access to the digital technology, physical distancing measures will be in place directing guests on how to move through the in-person check-in and check-out process in a safe way.

Tips for reading: English linking

- **consonant ⇔ vowel**

    We link words *ending with a consonant sound* to words *beginning with a vowel sound*

    we write it like this: turn off   Can I have a bit of egg?

    we read it like this: tur-noff   ca-<u>ni</u>-ha-<u>va</u>-bi-<u>to</u>-<u>v</u>egg?

- **vowel ⇔ vowel**

    We link words *ending with a vowel sound* to words *beginning with a vowel sound*

    we write it like this: pay all   the end   lie on   go out   too often

    we read it like this: pay$_y$all   the$_y$end   lie$_y$on   go$_w$out   too$_w$often

Part 2 Questions & Answers

Task One

Suppose you are a CUSTOMER who wants to book a room in the hotel. Read the following poster and you are required to ask 3 questions for detailed information.

The Jackson Hotel

Location: <u>Question 1</u>

Service: <u>Question 2</u>

Room rates: <u>Question 3</u>

Show your room key for discounts at
participating clubs and restaurants

Useful sentences for questions

- **ask for place**

  Where is ...?

  Where is the ... located?

  What is the location of ...?

- **ask for service**

  What is the service do you offer/provide?

  What room service can I get?

  Can I ... in your hotel?

- **ask for price**

  What are the rates of your hotel?

  What is the price of your rooms?

Unit 5

Task Two

Based on the same poster, read the following dialogue between the receptionist and customer. Suppose you are the receptionist, while reading, you are required to complete the conversation by answering the customer's questions.

The Jackson Hotel

Downtown location
Close to shopping & entertainment
Restaurants and coffee shops nearby
Free morning coffee and tea
Internet access in room
Fax services available
Room rates:
Single $68 Double $78, Extra person $18
Show your room key for discounts at
participating clubs and restaurants

Receptionist: The Jackson Hotel. Can I help you?

Customer: I'm going to spend my holiday in New York and I know from my friends about your hotel. Can you tell me some more information?

Receptionist: Yes, please.

Customer: Where is your hotel located?

Receptionist: _____.

Customer: What services do you provide?

Receptionist: _____.

Customer: Then what are the rates of your hotel?

Receptionist: _____.

Customer: That sounds good. I want a single room for next weekend, under the name of Mr. Black.

Receptionist: Good. I'll book the room for you. Thank you for calling. Bye.

Customer: Bye.

 **Part 3 Chinese-English Interpretation**

Task: In this part, you are required to translate a short speech into English orally.

先生们女士们，下午好。欢迎您乘坐中国东方航空公司航班MU587前往纽约。现在客舱乘务员将进行飞行前安全检查，请您系好安全带，打开遮阳板，并确认所有电子设备已关闭。在飞机起飞和下降过程中请不要使用手机和电脑。本次航班全程禁烟，在飞行途中请不要吸烟。本次航班的乘务长李勇将协同机上所有乘务员竭诚为您提供及时周到的服务。祝您旅途愉快，谢谢！

Useful sentences

- Morning, sir. Welcome aboard. Business class or economy?
- Follow me, please. Your seat is in the middle of the cabin.
- The plane is about to take off. Please don't walk about in the cabin.
- Flight No. 926, leaving Tokyo at 17:40, flies nonstop back to Beijing.
- Fasten your seat belts immediately. The plane will make an emergency landing because of the sudden breakdown of an engine.
- You know the weather in Hongkong is not so good. It has been delayed.

Unit 5

Part 4 Presentation

Task: In this part, you are required to talk about what is shown in the following bar graphs, describing and summarizing its contents. You should add your own comments.

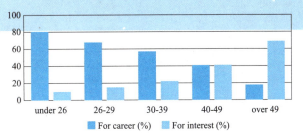

Reasons for Study according to age of student

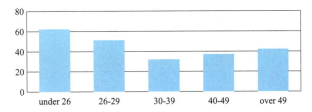

Employer support, by age group(%) (Time off and help with fees)

Main reasons for study among students of different age groups and the amount of support they received from employers

Useful sentences:

- for the beginning

  According to the table/pie chart/line graph/bar graph, we can see/conclude that …

  The table/graph reveals (shows/indicates/illustrates/represents/points out) that …

  As we can see from the table …

  As can be seen from the line/bar graph …

  As is shown (illustrated/indicated) in the pie chart …

- for describing changes

  Compared with … is still increased by …

  The number of … grew/rose from … to …

91

An increase is shown in …; then came a sharp increase of …

In … the number remains the same/drops to …

There was a very slight (small/slow/gradual) rise/increase in 1990.

There was a very steady (marked/sharp/rapid/sudden/dramatic) drop (decrease/decline/fall/reduction) in 1998/ compared with that of last year

Unit 5

Words List

1. location [ləʊˈkeɪʃn]	n.	地方，地点；位置；（电影的）外景拍摄地；定位
2. entertainment [ˌentəˈteɪnmənt]	n.	娱乐片；文娱节目；表演会；娱乐活动；招待；款待；娱乐
3. participate [pɑːˈtɪsɪpeɪt]	v.	参加；参与
4. aboard [əˈbɔːd]	adv./prep.	在（船、飞机、公共汽车、火车等）上；上（船、飞机、公共汽车、火车等）
5. cabin [ˈkæbɪn]	n.	（轮船上工作或生活的）隔间；（飞机的）座舱；（通常为木制的）小屋，小棚屋
	vi.	把……关在小屋里；使受拘束住在小屋里
6. emergency [iˈmɜːdʒənsi]	n.	突发事件；紧急情况
7. illustrate [ˈɪləstreɪt]	v.	加插图于；给（书等）做图表；（用示例、图画等）说明，解释；表明……真实；显示……存在
8. compare [kəmˈpeə(r)]	v.	比较；对比；与……类似（或相似）；表明……与……相似；将……比作
9. remain [rɪˈmeɪn]	v.	仍然是；保持不变；剩余；遗留；继续存在；仍需去做（或说、处理）
10. available [əˈveɪləbl]	adj.	可获得的；可购得的；可找到的；有空的

Practice after the unit

Exercise 1　Complete the following dialogue

Reservationist(R):　Good afternoon. Jackson Hotel. _____ (我能帮您什么吗)?

Client (C):　　　Good afternoon. I'm calling from Beijing Foreign Trade Company. Is it possible for me to have a suite?

R: Certainly, _____ (可以告诉我您的名字吗), sir?

C: West, W-E-S-T.

R: Thank you, Mr. West. But by the way, how long will you stay here?

C: I'll stay here for quite a long time.

R: I'm glad you will be staying at our hotel for a long time.

C: _____ (请问套房多少钱呢), please?

R: Your suite is 320 yuan (RMB) per day.

C: _____ (我需要提前预付吗)?

R: Yes, you may pay half of it. The account will be settled later.

C: That's fine.

R: Thank you, Mr. West. You have made a reservation for about 20 days at Jackson Hotel. We look forward to serving you.

C: Fine, thank you. Good-bye.

Exercise 2　Translate the following sentences into English:

1. 我想要预订一个单人间/双人间/豪华套间。
2. 是以谁的名义预订的房间？
3. 我想预订三天的标准间。
4. 你们酒店现在有空房吗？
5. 你们九点有接车服务吗？
6. 我们每天从早上 6 点到 9 点有免费的早餐自助餐，房价 150 元。

Unit 5

Reference answers

Part 2

Task One

Question 1　Where is your hotel?
Question 2　What Services do you procide?
Question 3　What are the rates of your hotel?

Task Two

1. It is in the downtown, close to shopping and entertainment center. There are restaurant and coffee shops nearby.
2. We offer morning coffee and tea for free. Internet access is in your room and fax services are provided in our hotel.
3. Let me check the room rates, 68 dollars for each single room, 78 dollars for each double room, 18 dollars will be added for one extra person.

Part 3

　　Good afternoon, ladies and gentlemen. Welcome aboard China Eastern Airlines flight MU587 from Shanghai to New York City. Now the cabin crew will make pre-flight safety check. Please fasten your seat belt, open the window shade, and make sure all electronic devices have been switched off. Thank you! Cell phones and laptop computers are not allowed to use during take-off and landing. This is a non-smoking flight; please do not smoke on board. The chief purser Li Yong with all crew members will be sincerely at your service. We hope you enjoy the flight. Thank you!

Part 4

　　The information given by the bar charts is about the major causes of study among students in different age group and the amount of support they acquired from employers.

The first graph shows that there is a gradual decrease in study for career reasons with age. Nearly 80% of students under 26 years study for their career. This percentage declines by 10% -20% every decade. Only 40% of 40-49 year olds and 18% of over 49 year olds are studying for career reasons. Conversely, there are only 10% of under 26 yr olds studying out of interest. The figure increases till the beginning of the fourth decade, and increases in late adulthood. However, 70% of over 49yr olds study for interest, about 4 times as many as that for career.

The second graph shows that employer support is maximum (about 60%) for the under 26yr students. It drops rapidly to 32% up to the third decade of life, and then increases in late adulthood up to about 44%. It is unclear whether employer support is only for career-focused study, but the highest level is for those students who mainly study for career purposes.

All in all, it is clear to see that there is an obvious difference in the distribution of reasons for study according to age group and most employers would like to give younger staff members time off and fees to continue academic study.

Unit 5

Bilingual Reading Time

Tips at Hotels
酒店小费

Hotel workers depend on tips to augment their usually small salaries. Rather than being annoyed at having to tip the doorman who greets you, consider it part of the cost of travel and be prepared with the dollar bills you will need to hand out before you even get to your room.

饭店的工作人员主要靠小费来增加他（她）们平时微薄的收入。不要对付给服务员小费感到愤愤不平，而应该把它看作旅游消费的一部分，并应做好在进入饭店之前就掏出钞票的准备。

Doormen

Depending on the amount of luggage, tip $1 to $2 to the doorman who takes your bags and turns them over to a bellman. If you are visiting and have no luggage, you naturally do not tip him for simply opening the door for you. Tip him again when you leave with your luggage as he takes it from the bellman and assists you in loading it in your car or into your taxi. When the doorman obtains a taxi for you, tip him $1 to $3 (the higher amount if he must stand in the rain for a period of time to get it).

门童

根据行李的数量，给门童 1 到 2 美元的小费，门童接过您的行李并将其交给行李员。如果你没有行李，通常就不必为他们只为你开门这样简单的服务付费。当你带着行李准备离开饭店而门童从行李员手中接过行李并帮你把它放入你的车子或出租车里时，你还应该付给他小费。当门童为你叫了一辆出租车时，你应该付他 1 至 3 美元（如果他为了叫辆出租车而不得不在雨中站着时，你的小费应该给得更多些。）

Bellman

Tip $1 a bag but not less than $2 to the bellman who carries or delivers your luggage to your room. When the bellman does something special for you, such as make a purchase or bring something you have requested to your room, but not room service deliveries, he or she should be tipped $2 to $3 for every service, at the time it is provided.

行李员

一个行李包要付 1 美元的小费，但对于把行李送到客房的行李员要付给 2 元以上的小费。当行李员为你做了一些特殊的事情，比如替你购物或把你需要的东西送到客房（但不属于客房服务范畴）等，他应该得到 2 至 3 美元的小费。

Maid

For stays of one night or more, the maid should be tipped $2 per night per person in a large hotel; $1 per night per person in a less expensive hotel. Give the maid her tip in person, if she can be found. If not, put it in a sealed envelope marked "chambermaid".

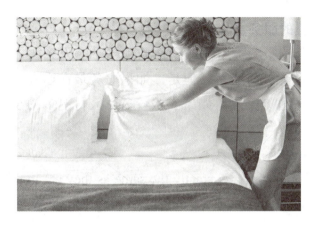

清理房间的女服务员

在一个较大、较豪华的饭店,清理房间的女服务员每人每天应得到 2 美元的小费;档次次之的饭店的服务员每人每天可得 1 美元小费。你可以亲自给她们小费,也可以把钱装在信封里封好,上面写明"送给清理房间的服务员"。

Valet

Valet services are added to your bill, so there is no need to tip for pressing or cleaning when items are left in your room. If you are in when your cleaning and pressing is delivered, however, tip $ 1 for the delivery for one or two items, more when several items are being delivered.

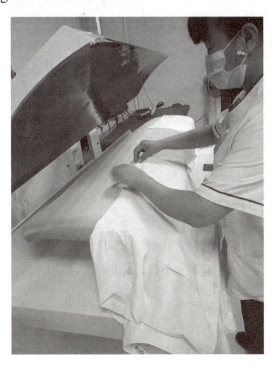

清洗、熨烫衣服的服务员

清洗、熨烫衣服的服务费用被加到你的账单中，因此如果在你外出的时候将衣服放在房间内你就无须付小费。但是，如果服务员在送衣服时你在房间内，可以为他们的送衣服务付1美元。如果衣服较多就应付更多的小费。

Dining Room Staff

Tips for dining room staff are exactly the same as they are in any other restaurant—15 to 18 percent except in the most elegant dining rooms where tips are 18 to 20 percent. If you are staying in an American plan hotel where your meals are included in your total bill, tips are as usual, and an additional tip should be given to the maitre'd who has taken care of you during your stay. This tip ranges anywhere from $ 10 to $ 15 for a weekend for a family or group of four people to $ 20 to $ 30 for a longer stay or larger group. (Extracted from kekenet.com)

餐厅服务员

付给饭店餐厅服务员的小费数目与其他餐馆服务员所得小费的数目不相上下，都是15%～18%，而一些非常豪华、档次最高的餐厅小费要高达18%～20%。如果你入住的饭店是餐费已包含于总账单的美式饭店，则小费还是15%～18%，并应向在您入住期间一直服务您的服务员提供额外的小费。如果一个家庭或一行四人要在此饭店住一星期的话，他们付出的小费从10美元至15美元不等，而在住宿的时间更长或人数更多的情况下，小费要达到20美元甚至30美元之多。

Unit 6

Visiting a Company

Warming-up

A. Match the following words with the corresponding pictures:

| headquarter | new products | branch office |
| establish business relations | department | joint venture |

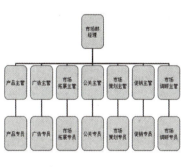
1. _____

2. _____

3. _____

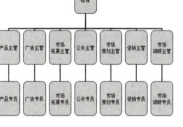
4. _____

5. _____

6. _____

B. Use the above words to complete the following sentences:

1. It consists of 4_____.
2. Our company _____ in Shanghai.
3. Look , they are our _____.
4. Our company is a Sino-American_____.
5. _____ between us will be our mutual benefit.
6. We have _____ in Hangzhou and Suzhou.

Unit 6

Part 1 Reading Aloud

Task: Read the following passage aloud

Ladies and gentlemen, It's a great honor to have you visit us today. I'm very pleased to have the opportunity to introduce our company to you.   Our company was established in 1997. We mainly manufacture electronic goods and export them all over the world. We grossed about US $150 million last year, and our business is growing steadily. We have offices in Asia, North America and Europe, with about 800 employees, and we are working gladly to serve the needs of our customers. In order to further develop our overseas market, we need reliable agents to promote our products. I hope you will consider doing business with us. Thank you.

Examine Tips

When reading English words, we should pay attention to the pronunciation of vowel and consonant, meanwhile master the relevant skills:

monophthong:

/ɑː/   /ɔː/   /ɜː/   /iː/   /uː/   /æ/
/ʌ/   /ɒ/   /ə/   /ɪ/   /ʊ/   /e/

Diphthong:

/eɪ/   /aɪ/   /ɔɪ/   /əu/
/au/   /eə/   /ɪə/   /uə/

Voiceless consonant:

/p/   /t/   /k/   /f/   /s/   /θ/   /ʃ/   /tʃ/   /tr/   /ts/   /h/

Voices consonant:

/b/   /d/   /g/   /v/   /z/   /ð/   /ʒ/   /dʒ/   /dr/   /dz/   /r/   /l/   /m/   /n/   /ŋ/   /w/   /j/

Part 2 Questions & Answers

Task One

Suppose you want to participate in the party. Read the following poster and you are required to ask 3 questions for detailed information.

Business English: Making Presentations
University of Washington

Starting date: Question 1

Deadline: flexible

English level required: intermediate

Hours suggested per week: 4 hours

Instructor: Question 2

Course learning objectives:

   1) to present information in an organized and engaging way;

   2) to share data in charts and graphs;

   3) to use persuasive language in a presentation

Final task: to develop a presentation that sells your city as a venue

Enrollment fee: Question 3

For more information, visit: onlinecourse@abc.com

- Suppose you are interested in the course advertised.
- You will have 1 minute to read through the poster SILENTLY.
- Then, you are required to ask 3 questions for detailed information.
- You will have 10 seconds to finish each question.

Unit 6

Question 1:
Question 2:
Question 3:

Task Two

Starting date: December 18, 2019
Deadline: flexible
English level required: intermediate
Hours suggested per week: 4 hours
Instructor: Richard Moore
Course learning objectives:
　　1) to present information in an organized and engaging way;
　　2) to share data in charts and graphs;
　　3) to use persuasive language in a presentation
Final task: to develop a presentation that sells your city as a venue
Enrollment fee: free
For more information, visit: onlinecourse@abc.com

- Now, you will hear a conversation with some parts missing. This conversation is between a man and a woman.
- Suppose you are the woman.
- While listening, you are required to complete the conversation by answering the man's questions.

W: Hi, Mike. Haven't seen you for a long time. How do you like your new job?
M: Not too bad. I'm thinking of improving my presentation skills. Any suggestions?
W: What about the online business presentation course offered by the University of Washington?
M: Sounds great. How many hours do I have to spend on the course every week?
W: _____1_____.
M: I see. By the way, what is the requirement of the English level?
W: _____2_____.

105

M: But I wonder if I can meet the deadline of the course.

W: No worries. You can reset the deadlines according to your own schedule.

M: That's good. Then what's the final task I will have to fulfill?

W: _____3_____.

M: It seems a bit difficult. Anyhow, I will have a try.

W: If you need to learn more about the course, you can visit its website.

M: OK. Thank you, Linda.

Examine Tips

We should master the using methods of interrogative pronoun and adverb:

what（什么）

who（谁，作主语）

which（哪个，在一定范围内选择）

whose（谁的，指附属关系）

whom（谁，作宾语）

when（何时，询问时间）

where（何地，询问地点）

why（为什么，询问原因）

how（如何，询问手段，方式，工具以及程度）

Unit 6

 Part 3 Chinese-English Interpretation

Task: In this part, you are required to translate a short speech into English orally.

这是我们的办公大楼。我们这里有所有的行政部门，比如销售部、会计部、人事部、市场调查部等。对面是仓库，成品存放在那里。仓库占地 2 600 平方米，去年我们安装了一条新的传送带。

Useful sentences for visiting a company

- I would like to make a brief introduction to our company.
- It sells best in many big cities all over China and recently has been exported to America and Europe.
- It has a history of 40 years, which makes in the oldest clothing company in our city.

Part 4 Presentation

Task: In this part, you are required to talk about what is shown in the following diagram, describing and summarizing its contents. You should add your own comments.

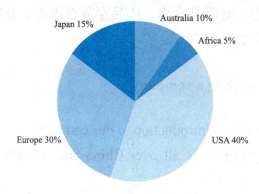

Market Share of MEX Company Products

Tips:

① 动词"占"的表达：

account for, hold, make up, take up, constitute, comprise, represent

② 百分比的表达

percentage，proportion, share, rate

③ 约数表达

the majority of, most of, a considerable number of, a minority of , just over…, slightly more than…/less than…, nearly half…

Useful sentences patterns：

— Asia accounts for almost a half of world population.

— Nearly 50% of people in the world come from Asia.

— China takes the lead in world population.

— Next comes food, whose percentage is higher than that of clothing.

— People seem to show no interest in reference books, which lies last in the percentage.

Words List

1. headquater [ˌhɛdˈkwɔːtə]	n.	总部	v. 设立总部
2. branch [brɑːntʃ]	n.	分部，分支	
3. population [ˌpɒpjuˈleɪʃn]	n.	人口	
4. establish [ɪˈstæblɪʃ]	n.	建立，创立	
5. share [ʃeə(r)]	n.	份额，股份	
6. administrative [ədˈmɪnɪstrətɪv]	n.	行政	
7. personnel [ˌpɜːsəˈnel]	n.	职员	
8. install [ɪnˈstɔːl]	v.	安装	
9. romantic [rəʊˈmæntɪk]	adj.	浪漫的	
10. booming [ˈbuːmɪŋ]	adj.	蓬勃发展的	

Practice after the unit

Exercise 1   Ask questions about the underlined parts:

1. Mr. Green is from <u>America.</u>
2. Amy's mother likes <u>romantic movies</u>.
3. His favorite sport is <u>football.</u>
4. She is <u>my sister.</u>
5. <u>Helen</u> will hold the meeting tomorrow.
6. He calls to his mother <u>once a week</u>.

Exercise 2   Translate the following sentences into English:

1. 我们目前有 900 名员工。
2. 我们注册资金为 8 000 万人民币。

3. 目前我们的市值达一亿人民币。
4. 我想知道更多关于贵公司的成长历史。
5. 它有40年历史,这使它成为我们市历史最悠久的服装公司。
6. 我想了解一些贵公司的企业管理文化,
7. 这里的每个员工都是我们组织的一分子。我们尊重每一个人,并且公平对待他们。

Unit 6

Reference answers

Part 2

Task One

Question 1: what is the starting date?
Question 2: who is the instructor?
Question 3: how much is the enrollment fee?

Task Two

1. 4 hours.
2. Intermediate
3. You have to develop a presentation that sells your city as a venue

Part 3

Now this is our office block. We have all the administrative departments here, for example, Sales, Accounting, Personnel, and Market Research and so on. The opposite one is the warehouse where the finished goods are stored. It covers an area of 2,600 square meters, and we installed a new conveyor belt last year.

Part 4

This pie chart shows the breakdown of the market share of MEX Company products in the world. As you can see, the U.S.A. is still our largest customer. It has the largest percentage of the market share of our products, at 40%. The second is Europe, at 30%. Next is Japan, which makes up 15% of our market share. And Australia accounts for 10%. Finally, the smallest part of our market share is taken up by Africa, with only 5%. Recently the world economy is not booming very fast, so we should improve our management system and try our best to produce better products and explore potential market in the future.

Bilingual Reading Time

Etiquette of Escort Visit
陪同参观的礼仪

Nowadays, our country continuously strengthens the contact with foreign countries in all aspects. The number of foreign companies, joint ventures and wholly owned enterprises who have investments in China continue increasingly, so the work that adapted to the foreign affairs communication and reception is more frequent. Before proceeding various forms of international economic cooperation and preparing for the decision-making and cooperation, many foreign guests will visit the partner's enterprise or company first, in order to get to know the situation in all aspects. When receive this kind of foreign guests, it is important to note all kinds of manners.

现今我国不断加强与国外各方面的联系。在华投资的外国公司、合资企业、独资企业不断增多，适应外事沟通接待的工作更加频繁。在进行各种经济合作，以及准备做决策或合作之前，许多外宾会先到合作方企业或公司参观，了解各方面的情况。接待这类外宾时，要注意各种礼仪。

Generally, you should explain the situations while accompany foreign guests to see around. The main conditions should be introduced by the leaders in person. When introducing the situations, make sure the words are concise and vivid, seek truth from facts, not false or exaggerated. When foreigners actively talk and shake hands with our employees during the visit, all people should greeted with enthusiasm, and disregard is forbidden as required.

一般情况下，陪同外宾参观时应说明情况。主要情况由领导亲自介绍。在介绍情况时，要做到言简意赅、实事求是，不虚假、不夸张。来访期间，外国人主动与我公司员工交谈、握手时，员工应热情迎接，不得漠视。

The guest's reaction and emotion should always be taken care during the visit. Do not speak alone. When guests ask questions, especially some tough questions, you should keep calm and answer them with smile in a humorous way. Do not show disgust emotion. For some principle problems, you should answer them cautiously, not randomly.

在参观过程中应始终关注客人的反应和情绪。不要与其单独说话。当客人提出问题，特别是一些棘手的问题时，应该保持冷静，用幽默的方式微笑回答。切不要表现出厌恶的情绪。而对于一些原则性问题，作答时应该谨慎，不得随意回答。

Pay more attention to the guests who stay behind for a long time just because of some individual part of interested. To send someone to take care of them, in case the guests are not neglected.

在陪同外宾参观的过程中,对那些因对个别之处感兴趣停留时间过长而落在后面的外宾。一定要派专人照顾,以免冷落对方。

At the end of the visit or on the way, people usually take pictures. Do not avoid or dodge when you take pictures with the foreign guests, just naturally accept the shoot. When taking group photos, the main leader and the head of visiting group should stand in the middle of the first row together and be sure to avoid touching each others' hand or shoulder.

在参观结束或途中,人们通常会拍照。与外宾合影时要大方自然,不要刻意回避或躲闪。集体拍照时,主要领导和参观团团长应站在第一排中间,并注意避免碰触对方的手或肩膀。

Unit 7

Vacation

Warming-up

A. Match the following words with the corresponding pictures:

| harvest   worship   couplets   flag   accompany   celebrate |

1. _____

2. _____

3. _____

4. _____

5. _____

6. _____

B. Use the above words to complete the following sentences:

1. It's a tradition of Spring Festival to paste _____.
2. Parents should spare some time to _____ their children no matter how busy they are.
3. Farmers are extremely busy during the _____.
4. Let's go out to a restaurant to _____.
5. I really _____ her serious attitude towards work.
6. The _____ is flying in the sky.

Unit 7

Part 1 Reading Aloud

Task: Read the following passage aloud

Good afternoon, ladies and gentlemen. I am delighted to introduce one of my favorite traditional Chinese festivals. Mid-autumn Festival, also called the Moon Festival, is always in September or October, on the 15th day of the 8th Chinese lunar calendar.

On that day, my family members get together and have a big dinner. After dinner, we traditionally offer sacrifices to the moon, in the belief that the moon will bring us good luck. The offerings may include mooncakes and fruits. If the weather is fine, we will appreciate the bright moon while eating mooncakes.

In the past, the Moon Festival was celebrated at harvest time. Ancient Chinese emperors worshiped the moon in autumn to thank it for the harvest. The ordinary people took Mid-Autumn Festival as a celebration of their hard work and harvest. Today, people mainly celebrate the moon festival as a time for family reunions.

Examine Tips

There are three major differences between British English and American English:
- Pronunciation-differences in both vowel and consonants, as well as stress and intonation;
- Vocabulary-differences in nouns and verbs, especially phrasal verb usage and the names of specific tools or items;
- Spelling-differences are generally found in certain prefix and suffix forms.

Part 2 Questions & Answers

Task One

Suppose you want to have a holiday. Read the following poster and you are required to ask 3 questions for detailed information.

Holiday Plans

Time: National Day
Destination: Question 1
Transport: Question 2
Duration: Five days
Activities: Climbing the Great Wall, watching the raising of the national flag on Tian'anmen Square, tasting Beijing duck, and so on.
Contact: Question 3
Website: www.travel.com

Task Two

Based on the same poster for holiday plans, read the following dialogue between two friends, Wang Lili(W) and Li Lei(L). Suppose you are Li Lei, while reading, you are required to complete the conversation by answering Wang Lili's questions.

Holiday Plans

Time: National Day
Destination: Beijing
Transport: By plane
Duration: Five days
Activities: Climbing the Great Wall, watching the raising of the national flag on Tian'anmen Square, tasting Beijing duck, and so on.
Contact: Local travel agency
Website: www.travel.com

Unit 7

W: Hi Li Lei. The National Day holiday is just around the corner. Do you have any plans?

L: Hi Wang Lili. I'm going to visit Beijing with my friends.

W: That's great. Beijing is a wonderful place to spend holidays. My dad has been there on business twice. How will you get there?

L: We're going to take a direct flight.

W: How long are you staying there?

L: _____

W: What are you going to do there?

L: Well, _____ By the way, how long does it take to fly to Beijing?

W: About three hours, I suppose. You can contact local travel agency.

L: Good idea. Do you know which website I can visit for more information?

W: _____

L: Thanks very much.

Examine Tips

- Read the post carefully and guess the new words according to the topic;
- Holiday is usually associated with travelling, so we can ask time, destination, transport and so on;
- Listen to questions carefully and pay attention to interrogative words such as what, when, where, who, how and so on.

 # Part 3 Chinese-English Interpretation

Task: In this part, you are required to translate a short speech into English orally.

请允许我介绍一下中国的春节。春节，是中国人最重要的节日，然而中国人更喜欢将其称为过年，其中过具有"通过"的含义。

那什么是年呢？年源于一个古老的中国故事。据说年是一个可怕的怪物，它在除夕之日出现，偷东西、吃人等等。所以，人们会在除夕那天贴春联、放鞭炮，希望吓跑怪物。

春节期间，人们先去拜访长辈，再拜访亲朋好友，俗称"拜年"。孩子们最开心，因为他们会得到红包，也称作压岁钱。

Useful words and expressions of Chinese traditional festivals:

- 春节 the Spring Festival or Chinese New Year　贴春联 paste couplets　放鞭炮 set off firecrackers
- 元宵节 the Lantern Festival　赏花灯 enjoy beautiful lanterns　猜灯谜 guess lantern riddles　看舞狮 watch lion dance
- 清明节 Qingming Festival or Tomb-sweeping Day　扫墓 sweep tombs　祭祖 worship ancestors
- 端午节 Dragon Boat Festival　粽子 Zongzi or rice dumpling　赛龙舟 dragon boat racing　纪念屈原 commemorate Qu Yuan　挂艾草 hang wormwood leaves
- 中秋节 the Mid-autumn Festival　月饼 mooncakes　团圆 reunion　赏月 appreciate the full moon

Unit 7

Part 4 Presentation

Task: In this part, you are required to talk about what is shown in the following graph, describing and summarizing its contents. You should add your own comments.

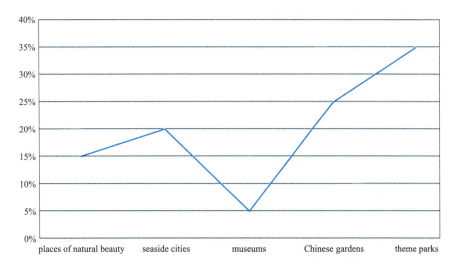

Survey about the kinds of places people like best for holidays

Useful sentences patterns:

- With the development of society/economy/education...
- A survey has been conducted about...
- As is shown in the graph
- On one hand...on the other hand...
- As far as I am concerned...
- In conclusion...

Practice after the unit

Exercise 1   Ask questions about the underlined parts:

1. I go to school <u>by bike</u>.

2. He likes <u>reading books</u> in his spare time.

3. Lucy plans to travel to <u>the UK</u> during the summer vacation.

4. They went to Shanghai <u>on National Day holiday</u>.

5. You can call <u>the manager</u> if you have problems.

Exercise 2   Translate the following sentences into English:

1. 请允许我介绍一下中国的传统节日。

2. 人们在元宵节赏花灯猜灯谜。

3. 据说端午节是为了纪念屈原。

4. 随着经济的发展，越来越多的人选择旅游来放松自己。

5. 一方面，旅游可以促进经济的发展。另一方面，旅游会给环境带来污染。

Words List

1. sacrifice ['sækrɪfaɪs] — *n.* 牺牲；祭品
2. appreciate [ə'priːʃi.eɪt] — *v.* 欣赏；感激
3. celebrate ['selə.breɪt] — *v.* 庆祝
4. harvest ['hɑː(r)vist] — *n.* 收获
5. ancient ['eɪnʃ(ə)nt] — *adj.* 古代的；古老的
6. emperor ['emp(ə)rə(r)] — *n.* 皇帝
7. worship ['wɜː(r)ʃɪp] — *v.* 崇拜；崇敬
8. reunion [riː'juːniən] — *n.* 团聚
9. flag [flæg] — *n.* 旗帜
10. around the corner — 即将到来

Unit 7

Reference answers

Part 2

Task One

Question 1 Where are you going?
Question 2 How will you go there?
Question 3 Who should I contact?

Task Two

Five days

We'll climb the Great Wall, watch the raising of the national flag on Tian'anmen Square, taste Beijing duck, and so on.

www dot travel dot com

Part 3

Please allow me to introduce the Spring Festival of China. The Spring Festival is the most important festival for Chinese people. However, Chinese people prefer to call it "guo nian", in which "guo" means pass-over.

Then what is the "nian"? Nian originated from an old Chinese story. It's said that Nian was a terrible monster. It appeared on the eve of the Spring Festival, stole things, ate people and so on. Therefore, people pasted couplets, set off firecrackers, hoping to scare away the monster.

During the Spring Festival, people visit the elderly first and then relatives and friends. This is what we say "bai nian". Children are the happiest because they can get red packets, which are also called gift money.

Part 4

With the development of the economy, more and more people begin to travel around to relax themselves. A survey has been conducted about the kinds of places people like best for holidays.

As is shown in the graph, 15% of the subjects choose places of natural beauty, 20% of them prefer seaside cities, 5% will go to museums. Also, many people like going to Chinese gardens and theme parks during holidays, which account for 25% and 35% respectively.

Nowadays theme parks have become the first choice when people plan holidays, such as the Disney Park and Ocean Park. One one hand, some thrilling activities can blow away people's stress and bring happiness to them. On the other hand, it's a good place for parents to accompany their children, and there are different kinds of activities which both adults and children can enjoy.

As far as I am concerned, I will spend my holiday in places of natural beauty. I'm a person who favors green hills and clear water. Surrounded in the world of nature, I can breathe fresh air, which will bring peace to either mind or body.

Unit 7

Bilingual Reading Time

Poolside working is no longer a sign of importance
高管新时尚：休假时不工作

When I was at university I spent a summer travelling around Europe with some friends, and one of them suggested we drop in on his parents' place in the south of France.

大学时的一个夏天，我和一群朋友一起环游欧洲，其中一个朋友邀请我们到法国南部他的父母家做客。

There are two things I remember about that visit. There was the mortification of being greeted by a butler who ceremoniously carried my tatty luggage — a few things stuffed into a plastic bag — to the suite of rooms to which I'd been allocated. But what stays in my mind even more was the image of his father — who turned out to be a famous tycoon — clad in small swimming trunks with cigar clamped between teeth, holding a gin and tonic in one hand and a telephone receiver in the other.

说起那次拜访，有两件事我至今记忆犹新。首先让我觉得很没面子的是，一名管家彬彬有礼地将我寒酸的行李——一只塞了许多东西的塑料包——送到为我安排的套房。而让我印象更为深刻的是我朋友父亲的样子——他原来是位有名的大亨——只见他穿着窄小的泳裤，嘴里叼着雪茄，一手端着杯金汤力，一手握着电话听筒。

The year was 1979 and this was what power looked like. The man was too important to be out of touch with the deals he was doing. So he had installed a telephone line by the swimming pool and passed his summers issuing instructions from a lounger by the water.

那时是1979年,当时大人物就是这样。这个男人位高权重,没法将自己的生意放手不管。所以他在泳池边也装上了电话,于是他在水边的躺椅上发号施令,度过了一个个夏日。

A quarter of a century later, technology allowed all of us to pretend to be tycoons. We might not have had the butler or the pool house but everyone could head to the beach with a BlackBerry packed along with their towels. And because we could, we did. Only for most of us, what we were doing was not deals, it was responding to mundane inquiries that could have waited two weeks — or forever.

25年过去了,技术使我们人人都能装成大亨。也许我们没有管家或是带泳池的房子,但都能带着浴巾和黑莓(BlackBerry)手机去海滩。正因为我们能这样做,我们就这样做。只不过我们多数人都不是在做生意,而是在回复鸡毛蒜皮的小事,这些事可以两周后再处理——或者干脆不用理会。

This year, I decided to do something radical that I hadn't done for almost a decade. I took a proper holiday. I disconnected myself from work altogether. I didn't open any work messages. I spent time reading, walking, looking at the sea — and sometimes getting into it — while I thought about not much at all. When I returned to work and reacquainted myself with email, it was perfectly straightforward. I deleted almost all of them unread, responding only to the things that looked interesting. Far from feeling overwhelmed, I felt a certain excitement in the sudden immersion in work. It was a new-shoes and sharp-pencil sort of feeling that used to go with the beginning of a school term.

今年,我决定做些大胆的尝试,我已经有将近十年没这样做了。我惬意地度了个假;全然抛开了工作,不去打开任何与工作有关的消息。我阅读、散步、瞭望大海——有时到海里泡一泡——脑子里什么都不想。回来上班后,我非常简捷地处理了电子邮件。我几乎删除了所有未读邮件,只回复那些看起来有趣的。突然恢复工作不仅没让我觉得不堪重负,反而让我有一点兴奋。这种感觉似曾相识,就像以前在新学期伊始，穿上新鞋子，削尖了铅笔的感觉。

Over the past week it has started to dawn on me that my radical action was not radical at all. I was merely following the latest fashion.

过去一周，我意识到自己的大胆举动其实一点都不大胆，仅仅是赶了趟时髦。

Last week I sent an email to an entrepreneur I know, and within seconds the automatic reply came back: "I am on holiday until August 30 and will not be checking messages." This was particularly remarkable given that last time I'd seen him — some five years ago — he had told me how he expected all his employees to respond to messages instantly wherever they were and whatever they were doing.

上星期，我给一位认识的企业家发了封邮件，随即就收到了自动回复："目前我正在休假，8月30日前不会查看信箱。"这种口吻跟我上次见到他时——大约五年前——简直判若两人。那时他对我说，他希望所有员工，不论何时何地，都能第一时间回复信息。

So I emailed back asking what had made him change his mind — but all I got in return was the same automatic message telling me he wasn't reading whatever I was sending.

于是，我回邮件问他为什么改变了想法——可收到的仍旧是一模一样的自动回复。无论我发什么，他都不会看。

The very next day I got an email from a woman who I had contacted before I went away. It began: "Sorry for my radio silence — I have had a blissful two-week holiday and am just catching up on emails on my return." Here was the same thing again: a driven, thirtysomething entrepreneur who wanted me to know not how hard she worked on holiday but how she loafed around, and how much she enjoyed it.

就在第二天，我在休假前联系过的一位女士给我发了封邮件。邮件开头这样写道："抱歉一直没回复，我度过了一个两周长的愉快假期，回来后才开始处理邮件。"这又是一个同样的事例，一个锐意进取、已届而立之年的企业家，想让我看到的不是她在假期如何努力工作，而是她如何放松，如何适得其乐。

To see how widespread this change is, I've done a little experiment. I've collected all the out-of-office emails I've had this summer, and counted the number that were followed at once by an email sent from the beach. Three years ago, it was very unusual for an automatic message not to be quickly followed by a real one. This year I've had a total of 38 automatic messages telling me the sender was away, only six of which have been succeeded by a personal, poolside reply.

为了看看这种变化有多普遍，我做了个小实验。我收集了今年夏天收到的所有外出时的自动应答邮件，又数了数那些在第一时间从海滩回复的邮件。三年前，收到一封自动回复邮件后，如果没有一封真实的邮件紧随其后，是很稀罕的。今年，我总共收到 38 封外出时的自动应答邮件，其中只有 6 封邮件随后有真人从泳池边上发来了回复。

Bragging about not working on holiday seems to be part of a wider trend — which I wrote about a few months ago — in which fashionable execs flaunt not their long hours, but their short ones. To be emailing from the pool does not prove you are powerful, it is starting to be seen for what it is — a sign of weakness, poor time management and an inability to delegate. If you can take two weeks off altogether, it shows you have overcome all gadget addiction, and like a modern-day tycoon can control when you work — and when you don't.

夸耀自己不在假期工作符合一种趋势：紧跟时代潮流的企业高管们炫耀的不再是花了很长时间工作，而是只用了很短时间就完成了工作——我几个月前曾写过一篇文章谈到了这种趋势。在泳池边发邮件并不能证明你有影响力，这开始被人们视为能力不足、不善管理时间以及不会放权的证明。如果你能休息整整两个星期，则说明你已经克服了对电子设备的依赖，而且像一个现代大亨一样，自己掌控着何时工作——何时不工作。

Unit 8

The Graduation Ceremony

Warming-up

A. Match the following words with the corresponding pictures:

| ceremony   graduate   evening party   certificate   performance hall   pie chart |

1. _____

2. _____

3. _____

4. _____

5. _____

6. _____

B. Use the above words to complete the following sentences:

1. The _____ can hold 300 audiences at most.
2. I'll _____ form Silicon Lake College in three years.
3. College students are required to get the _____ of Computer Rank Examination.
4. The _____ will be held in the _____ at 7:00 pm this evening.
5. It is a great honor for me to speak at the _____ on behalf of all graduates.
6. The _____ shows the different factors that students considered when choosing university

Unit 8

 Part 1 Reading Aloud

Good morning, my dear teachers and schoolmates. It's a great honor for me to make a speech on behalf of all graduating students.

How time flies! Our college lives will come to an end. Looking back on the first day that we came to the school, it is so vivid which feels like it just happened. The past three years has been really a wonderful journey, full of laughter and tears.

In the past three years, our great teachers contributed their time, energy, love and the whole heart on teaching us. We've learned a lot from them, not only knowledge but also the way to solve problems in life.

Thanks for our teachers' training, parents' support and the help from classmates. Without them, we couldn't have so much wonderful time.

Finally, on behalf of all the graduates present here, let me extend our sincere wishes for our mother school and respectable teachers and wish all our dreams will come true. Thank you for listening.

Tips:

When reading English, we should pay attention to the following rules of pronunciation:
- In some vocabularies, one or two letters don't sound, eg.: heir [eə], debt[det];
- Some words contain two vowels, which belong to different syllables instead of letter combinations. They should be pronounced with their own sounds, and the pronunciation should be as long as possible, eg.: radio['reɪdiəʊ], violate['vaɪəleɪt]];
- Some words have multiple sounds due to multiple meanings, eg.: desert ['dezət] n. 沙漠； desert [dɪ'zɜːt] v. 抛弃，离弃

Part 2 Questions & Answers

Task One

Suppose you want to participate in the event Read the following poster and you are required to ask 3 questions for detailed information.

Job Training Center

Participants: <u>Question 1</u>
Time: <u>Question 2</u>
Place: <u>Question 3</u>
Address: Room508, Fifth floor, 168 Greenland Avenue
Occupations: Interior Design, Environment Technician, Accounting, Logistics Management
Contact Person: John Smith, Job Training Management
Telephone Number: 57788001
Website: www.jobtraining.org

Useful questions:

1. Who are required to participate in the conference?
2. What time will the training begin?
3. Where will be the training located?
4. What is the address of the training center?
5. What kinds of training are offered?
6. Whom shall I contact if I want to know more information?
7. What number shall I dial if I want to sign in?
8. What is the website of the company?

Unit 8

Task Two

Based on the same poster for the New Year's recreation evening party, read the following dialogue between two friends, Wang Lili(W) and Li Lei(L). Suppose you are Wang Lili, while reading, you are required to complete the conversation by answering Li Lei's questions.

Job Training Center

Participants: Question 1

Time: Question 2

Place: Question 3

Address: Room508, Fifth floor, 168 Greenland Avenue

Occupations: Interior Design, Environment Technician, Accounting, Logistics Management

Contact Person: John Smith, Job Training Management

Telephone Number: 57788001

Website: www.jobtraining.org

W: Hi, Li Lei. You look worried. What's wrong with you?

L: I'm unemployed. And I've been trying hard to find a new job.

W: Why not take a training course? There is a free one for unemployed people in the city.

L: Really? When and where?

W: Every Tuesday at 10:00 a.m., at Silicon Lake Entrepreneurship Center.

L: But what is the address of the center?

W: _____.

L: What kinds of training are offered?

W: Quite a lot. I guess Interior Design is suitable for you.

L: Yes, I think so. But who should I contact?

W: _____.

L: I see. Have you got his telephone number?

W: Yes, it's 57788001.

L: By the way, what's the website that I can visit for more information?

W: _____.
L: Thank you.

Examine Tips

- Students should ask the questions in accordance with the contents of the poster, and answer the questions when hearing the hinting sound of the system;
- When preparing, students should read the poster carefully and understand all kinds of information that showed in the poster;
- When asking a question about "Participants", we should use special interrogative adverb of the who; When asking a question about "Time", we should use special interrogative adverb of the when; When asking a question about "Place", we should use special interrogative adverb of the where; we should choose different special interrogative adverb in accordance with different questions.

Unit 8

Part 3 Chinese-English Interpretation

Task: In this part, you are required to translate a short speech into English orally.

各位老师，各位同学，大家好!我是来自经济管理学院 2018 级的李雷，非常荣幸能作为毕业生代表发言。时光飞逝，三年的大学生活很快就过去了，学校的学习和生活为我们奠定了坚实的基础。明天我们就要离开曾经憧憬向往的大学生涯，走向我们的最终归宿——社会。服务社会才是我们的最终目标，我们会投身在社会的大课堂中不断进步，在社会的大舞台上大展宏图。再次，我代表全体毕业生，感谢母校三年来对我们的培养和教育，感谢各位领导和老师对我们的关爱和教诲，感谢家人对我们的付出和鼓励，感谢身边朋友带给我们的快乐和帮助。

Useful sentences:

1. I am _____ from the School of _____, in the Grade of _____.
2. It is a great honor for _____ to _____ as _____.
3. How time flies.
4. _____ have/has laid a solid foundation for _____.
5. _____ is the ultimate goal.
6. I would like to extend my thanks to _____.

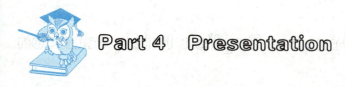

Part 4 Presentation

Task: In this part, you are required to:

1. describe the chart;
2. give your comments on the advantages and disadvantages of starting one's own career;
3. tell what you prefer to do after graduation.

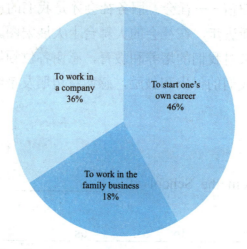

What Students Expect to Do After Graduation

Useful sentences patterns:

- To describe the content of the chart

    The diagram/chart/graphic shows that_____

    The data/figures/statistics show that _____

    The pie/bar chart depicts/illustrates (that) _____

    This is a curve graph which describe the general trend of _____

    The table shows the changing proportion of _____ from _____

- To describe the changes of the chart
  Over the period from _____ to _____, the _____ remained level.
  The percentage of _____ stayed the same between _____ and _____.
  The percentage of _____ is slightly larger/smaller than that of The percentage of _____.
  _____ decreased year by year while _____ increased steadily.
  A is _____ times as much/many as B.

- To draw a conclusion in accordance with the table
  As is shown/demonstrated/exhibited in the diagram/graph/chart/table, _____
  The graph reflects that _____
  The statistics lead us to the conclusion that _____
  According to the chart/figures, _____
  In a word, _____

Words List

1. graduate ['grædʒueɪt]　　　　　v.　　毕业
2. ceremony ['serəmoʊni]　　　　n.　　典礼
3. certificate [sə'tɪfɪkeɪt]　　　　n.　　证书
4. audience ['ɔːdiəns]　　　　　n.　　观众，听众
5. participant [pɑː'tɪsɪpənt]　　　n.　　参与者；参加者
6. occupation [ˌɒkju'peɪʃn]　　　n.　　工作；职业
7. performance [pə'fɔːməns]　　 n.　　表演，演出
8. behalf [bɪ'hɑːf]　　　　　　　n.　　代表
9. foundation [faʊn'deɪʃn]　　　n.　　基础
10. career [kə'rɪə(r)]　　　　　　n.　　职业，事业

Practice after the unit

Exercise 1   Ask questions about the underlined parts:

1. The conference room can hold <u>300 audiences</u>.

2. The evening party will be held <u>in the performance hall</u> this evening.

3. <u>Serving the society</u> is the ultimate goal.

4. The address of the center is <u>Room508，Fifth floor, 168 Greenland Avenue</u>.

5. You can contact <u>John Smith, Job Training Management</u>.

6. The training course will be given <u>on every Tuesday at 10:00 a.m.</u>.

Exercise 2   Translate the following sentences into English:

1. 明年七月我将大学毕业。

2. 我的专业是室内设计。

3. 毕业后我想要自己创业。

4. 我代表全体师生欢迎各位专家的到来。

5. 这项调查的目的是找出微信给人们的生活带来了哪些影响。

6. 近些年，越来越多的大学生毕业后选择自主创业。

Unit 8

Reference answers

Part 2

Task One

Question 1 Who can participate in the training?
Question 2 When will the training be held?
Question 3 Where will the training be held?

Task Two

Room508，Fifth floor, 168 Greenland Avenue
John Smith, Job Training Management
www.jobtraining.org

Part 3

Dear teachers and classmates, I am Li Lei from the School of Economics and Management, in the Grade of 2018. It is a great honor for me to make a speech as a representative of graduates. How time flies. The three-year college life has passed quickly. The three-year college life and study have laid a solid foundation for us. We will leave the campus which we once dreamed of and move towards our final destination—the society. Serving the society is our ultimate goal. We will devote ourselves to the social classroom, make continuous progress and achieve great achievements in the society. Again, on behalf of all graduates, I would like to extend my thanks to my alma mater for training and education in the past three years, to all the leaders and teachers for the cultivation and education in the past three years, as well as to the family members for their dedication and encouragement, and to the friends for the happiness and help.

Part 4

A survey has been conducted on students expect to do after graduation. The purpose is to find out what students expect to do after graduation.

Based on the survey, 46% of the subjects said that they would start their own career, 36% of them said that they would get a job in a company; there are also students would work in their family business, which account for 18%.

From the survey we can see that more students choose to start their own career after graduation. When starting one's own business, we will meet many challenges. First of all, as freshmen who have just entered the society, it is obvious that college graduates lack related experience, which will increase the rate of failure they may encounter during starting a career. Being short of entrepreneurial experience is one of the difficulties that college graduates need to overcome. In addition, the collection of money is another problem they should solve urgently. Otherwise, there is no possibility of starting a career. However, a person's comprehensive abilities will be greatly improved in the process of starting a career, because overcoming difficulties can only make people stronger. It's no exaggeration to say that starting a career is conducive to bringing one's potential and talents into full play.

As far as I am concerned, I prefer to start my own career after graduation, for I want to be my own boss and I can gain a lot of entrepreneurial experience.

Unit 8

Bilingual Reading Time

Five ways to make graduates to take a firm stand in the workplace
5 招让毕业生笑傲职场

The shift from college to real life can be a tough one, but if you're able to maintain a positive outlook, it can also be a fun, exciting time. Hoping to amp up your optimism and get ahead? You'll thrive during the postgrad transition by following these mood- boosting tips:

从校园生活到现实生活的转变过程可能会非常艰难，但是如果你能保持乐观的心态，这段时间也可以是充满乐趣、令人兴奋的。想要提升你的乐观情绪并取得进步吗？遵循以下这些能让你保持乐观情绪的建议，你将会在从校园到职场的转型期里茁壮成长。

Connect With Fellow Grads
和大学同学保持联系

After four years of roommates, cafeterias, and constant companions, the postgrad life can feel like an awfully lonely road. Feeling a little lost? Look for someone who truly understands what you're going through and reach out to friends who can offer an empathetic ear.

和大学的好伙伴们同吃同住同行度过了四年，毕业后的生活确实让人感觉十分寂寞。是否有些失落呢？找一个能真正理解你内心煎熬的朋友，也可以向那些和你有同感的朋友倾诉。

Build a Professional Network
建立一个职业网络

Finding a job can definitely be stressful, so make the task easier on yourself by establishing a strong network of young professionals. The more people you know, the more likely you are to have a valuable, job-securing connection. Begin by reaching out via Linked-In or Facebook, then send an email to friends and parents who may be able to help. Every little effort will make you feel productive and just a bit more self-assured.

找工作无疑会让你压力巨大，建立一个年轻专业人员的强大网络会让你的求职变得容易些。你认识的人越多，你就越有可能获得一种有价值的关系，这将有

助于你找到工作。刚开始可以在商务化人际关系网（Linked-In）或社交网络（Facebook）上寻找联系人，之后可以给可能会帮助你的朋友和父母发电子邮件。每一点努力都会让你感到成就感，也会让你多一份自信。

Learn From the Experts
向专家学习

Feeling defeated and uninspired? Do a bit of research to find local lectures related to your field. Attend panels, join job-related groups, and read as much as possible about the industry you hope to join. Taking a few (or several) steps in the right direction will reinvigorate your professional passions and kick-start your enthusiasm.

有挫败感，毫无创意？搜索一下，寻找当地和你的工作领域相关的讲座。出席专题讨论会，加入和工作相关的团体，并且尽可能多地阅读你渴望加入的产业相关的书籍。朝着正确的方向迈进几步会让你重燃职业激情，并且让你的热情迸发。

Remember to Look Forward
记住要向前看

It's only natural to get nostalgic every once in a while, but don't let yourself long for the glory days too often. Instead, map out your dream life. Decide where you want to be in five, 10, 15 years, then create an inspiration board to keep your eyes on the prize.

偶尔怀旧一下还算正常,但不要让自己总是沉湎于过去的光辉岁月。相反你应该筹划一下梦想的生活。决定未来的 5 年、10 年、15 年你想要成为什么样的人,然后制作一块鼓舞人心的标牌,一直盯着你可能收获的那些回报。

Take Steps Toward Your Goal
朝着目标步步为营

It's easy to say what you want, but real happiness comes from acting on that desire. Fantasize about your future as an event planner? Throw parties to showcase your talent, start a blog to build a following, and reach out to experts to find a mentor you respect. Gaining credibility is sure to strengthen your confidence, so you'll be back on the optimistic path in no time.

说出自己想要什么很容易,但真正的幸福来自为这种渴望付出的行动。像一名规划师那样幻想你的未来吗?举办聚会来展现你的才能,开通博客来吸引一群粉丝,多和专家接触来寻找你尊敬的良师益友。收获信誉度毫无疑问会增强你的自信心,这样你很快就会回归乐观的轨道。

The bottom line: Transitions aren't easy, so it's important to cut yourself some slack as you move through the grey area. Tuck away the scrapbooks for another time, and for now, just remember to stay connected, put yourself out there, and focus on the bright future that lies ahead of you.

结束语：从毕业生到职场人的转型并不容易，所以当你穿过这片灰色地带时，克服自身的懒散非常重要。把相册先收起来留着以后用，现在只要记住，保持和周围人的联系，勇敢地迈向职场，专注于摆在你面前的光明未来

第三部分

高等学校英语应用能力考试（口试）样题

PRACTICAL ENGLISH TEST FOR COLLEGES

ORAL
Candidate's Test Paper One

National Board of Practical English Test for Colleges

Warm-up Questions   (1.5 minutes)

Please read your name and your registration number to the microphone loudly when you see or hear the prompt.

[Prompt from the system]

---------------- [For your registration -- 10 seconds] ----------------

Now, here are some warm-up questions.

<u>Task</u>:

After you hear each question, there will be a pause. During the pause you should give your answer.

You should begin to answer the question when hearing the beginning signal sound and stop on hearing the ending signal sound.

Now please listen to the questions.

Question 1: [Please listen!]

[Timing begins]

---------------- **[Your answer please** -- 10 seconds] ----------------

[Timing ends]

Question 2: [Please listen!]

[Timing begins]

---------------- **[Your answer please** -- 10 seconds] ----------------

[Timing ends]

Question 3: [Please listen!]

[Timing begins]

---------------- **[Your answer please** -- 10 seconds] ----------------

[Timing ends]

This is the end of Warm-up questions.

Part I   **Aloud Reading**   (2.5 minutes)

In this part, there is a short text shown on the computer screen (as is shown below).

Task:

-- You are required to read aloud the text.

-- You'll have 1 minute for preparation.

-- Then, you are required to read aloud the text when hearing the beginning signal sound and stop on hearing the ending signal sound.

Your voice will be recorded into the system.

Now you have 1 minute to prepare. PLEASE READ SILENTLY!

[Timing begins]

---------------- [**Please read through silently**-- 1-minute pause] ----------------

Good afternoon, ladies and gentlemen. Our plane is about to depart from Beijing Airport for New York City. If you look at the card in your seat pocket, you will see where the emergency exits are located. In case of an emergency, an oxygen mask will come down from an overhead compartment. For overwater emergencies your life vest is under your seat. There is no smoking at any time on this flight. For takeoff, please put your seat in an upright position, lock your tray table, and turn off all electrical devices, including computers and cell phones, and be sure your seat belt is fastened. After takeoff, our crew will be serving beverages. Thank you.

[Timing ends]

Now please get ready to read aloud the text. Try to finish it within 1 minute.

[Timing begins]

---------------- [**Please read aloud** -- 1 minute] ----------------

[Timing ends]

This is the end of Part I.

Part II　　　　Questions & Answers　　　　(4 minutes)

In this part, you see a hotel advertisement shown on the computer screen (as is shown below). There are TWO tasks for you to finish.

THE FORD HOTEL

Downtown location

Close to shopping & entertainment

Restaurants and coffee shops nearby

Free morning coffee and tea

Internet access in room

Fax services available

Room rates:

Single $55, Double $65, Extra person $20

Show your room key for discounts at

participating clubs and restaurants

Task One:

-- Suppose you are a CUSTOMER who wants to book a room in the hotel.

-- You'll have 1 minute to read through the advertisement SILENTLY.

-- Then, you are required to ask 3 questions for more detailed information you are interested in, such as its location, service and rates.

-- You'll have 10 seconds to finish each question.

You should begin to ask questions on hearing the beginning signal sound and stop on hearing the ending signal sound.

Now, please silently read the advertisement above.

[Timing begins]

---------------- [Your silent reading please -- 1 minute] ----------------

[Timing ends]

Now, please get ready to ask questions.

[Timing begins]

Question 1:

---------------- [**Your question please** --10 seconds] ----------------

[Timing ends]

[Timing begins]

Question 2:

---------------- [**Your question please** -- 10 seconds] ----------------

[Timing ends]

[Timing begins]

Question 3:

---------------- [**Your question please** -- 10 seconds] ----------------

[Timing ends]

Task Two:
-- You will hear a gapped conversation between a receptionist and a customer who wants to book a room in the hotel.
-- Suppose you are the RECEPTIONIST.
-- While listening to the conversation you are required to complete the gap by answering the customer's questions.
-- You'll have 10 seconds to finish each answer.
You are required to answer questions on hearing the beginning signal sound and stop on hearing the ending signal sound.
Here is the gapped conversation recording. Remember to answer the question when you hear a signal sound.

Receptionist: ...?
Customer: ...?
Receptionist: ...?
Customer: ...?

[Timing begins]

Receptionist:

_____.

---------------- [**Please answer the question** -- 10 seconds] ----------------

[Timing ends]

Customer: ...?

[Timing begins]

Receptionist:

_____.

---------------- [**Please answer the question** -- 10 seconds] ----------------

[Timing ends]

Customer: ...?

[Timing begins]

Receptionist:

_____.

---------------- [**Please answer the question** -- 10 seconds] ----------------

[Timing ends]

Customer: ....

Receptionist: ....

Customer: ....

This is the end of Part II.

Part III   Chinese-English Interpretation   (3 minutes)

In this part, there is a telephone conversation text shown on the computer screen (as is shown below). Part of it is in English and part in Chinese.

Task:

-- You are required to ORALLY interpret the Chinese part into English.

-- First, you'll have 30 seconds to prepare. Then, you should begin to ORALLY interpret when hearing the beginning signal sound and stop on hearing the ending signal sound. You'll have another 1.5 minutes to finish the task.

Now you have 30 seconds to prepare.

[Timing begins]

---------------- [**For your preparation** -- 30 seconds] ----------------

Answering Machine: Hi. You have reached the Johnson's. We can't come to the phone now, but if you leave your name, number, and a brief message at the sound of the beep, we'll get back to you as soon as we can.

Jack: 我是杰克，我要给约翰逊夫人留言。很抱歉这个星期五晚上我不能去车站接您了。不过如果您同意的话，我的一个朋友愿意帮忙。她叫玛丽。她的电话号码是892-22233。

[Timing ends]

[30 seconds later]

Now, please get ready to interpret orally.

[Timing begins]

---------------- [**Your interpretation please** -- 1.5 minutes] ----------------

[Timing ends]

This is the end of Part Ⅲ.

Part Ⅳ　　　　　Presentation　　　　　(4 minutes)

In this part, a trade record of import and export of MAX Company is shown on the computer screen (as is shown below).

Task:

-- You are required to talk about the figure, describing, comparing and summarizing the changes of its imports and exports. You can add your own opinions.

-- You should begin to speak when hearing the beginning signal sound and stop on hearing the ending signal sound.

You'll have 1 minute to prepare and another 2 minutes to complete your presentation.

Now you have 1 minute to prepare.

[Timing begins]

---------------- [**For your preparation** - 1 minute] ----------------

[Timing ends]

[1 minute later]

Now, please get ready to give your presentation.

[Timing begins]

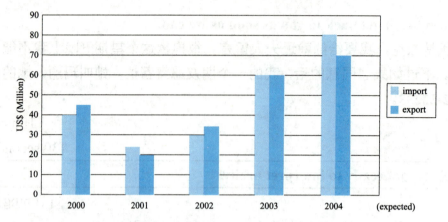

Foreign Trade Record of MAX Company

---------------- [**Your presentation please** -- 2 minutes] ----------------

[Timing ends]

This is the end of Part Ⅳ.

And also, this is the end of the test. Thank you.

第四部分

口语补充对话

(1) Introductions and Opening Conversations

People in the United States don't always shake hands when they are introduced to one another. However, in a formal or business situation people almost always shake hands.

1. A: Mary, this is Joe's brother David.

   B: I'm very glad to meet you.

   C: It's a pleasure to meet you.

   B: How do you like Texas so far?

   C: It's really different from what I expected.

   B: Don't worry. You'll get used to it in no time.

2. A: Mrs. Smith, I'd like to introduce a friend of mine, Pierre Dubois.

   B: How do you do?

   C: Hello.

   B: What's your impression of the United States?

   C: Well, I can't get over how different the weather is here.

   B: Oh, you'll get used to it soon!

(2) Special Greetings

There are eight national holidays celebrated in the United States: New Year's Day(Jan.), Washington's Birthday (Feb.), Memorial Day(May), the Fourth of July, Labor Day(Sep.),Veteran's Day(Nov.),Thanksgiving(Nov.) and Christmas(Dec.), In addition, there are many state and local holidays.

1. A: Merry Christmas!

   B: The same to you!

   A: Are you doing anything special?

   B: We're having some friends over. What are you doing?

   A: Oh, I'm just going to take it easy.

2. A: Happy New Year!

   B: Thank you! Same to you.

   A: Have you got any plans?

   B: I've been invited over to la friend's. And you?

   A: My roommate's having a party.

(3) Meeting old friends

Many people shake hands when meeting after they haven't seen each other for a long time.

1. A: I haven't seen you for ages. You haven't been rich, have you?
   B: No, I've been in California for the past month.
   A: How nice. Where were you exactly?
   B: San Diego. I got back yesterday.
2. A: It's nice to see you again. Have you changed jobs?
   B: No, I've been visiting relatives.
   A: That's nice. Where?
   B: I went to visit an uncle of mine in San Francisco.

(4) Saying Goodbye

When you're far from friends and family, you can keep in touch with them by letters, post cards, short notes or phone calls.

1. A: I've come to say goodbye.
   B: When are you off?
   A: I'm flying home on Sunday afternoon.
   B: Well, goodbye. See you soon.
   A: Please don't forget to say goodbye to the rest of the family for me.
2. A: I'd like to say goodbye to everyone.
   B: What time are you going?
   A: My plane leaves at 7:25.
   B; Well, goodbye and have a good trip!
   A: Goodbye. Remember to look me up if you're ever in Washington.

(5) Saying Thank You

When someone invites you for dinner, you can bring flowers, candy or a bottle of wine. Sometimes people send a thank you note to the host or hostess a few days after the event.

1. A: I'd better be going.
   B: So soon? Why don't you stay a little longer?
   A: I wish I could, but it's already late.

B: Oh, it's a shame that you have to leave.

A: Thank you for a wonderful meal.

B: I'm glad you enjoyed it.

2. A: I really must be going now.

B: But you just got here. Can't you stay a little longer?

A: That's very nice of you, but I really can't.

B: Well, it's too bad that you have to go.

A: Thanks very much. It was a great party!

B: It was our pleasure.

(6) Asking People to Repeat

As long as you ask politely, most people do not mind repeating something you didn't hear or understand.

1. A: I'm sorry, but I didn't catch what you said.

B: I said, "Do you want me to help you?"

A: If you're sure you're not in a hurry, I can use a little help.

B: Would you like me to get you a cab?

2. A: I beg your pardon?

B: I said, "Do you need any help?"

A: That's very nice of you. I guess I could use some help.

B: Just tell me what you'd like me to do.

(7) Asking Favors

When you ask for things, it is important to be polite. The intonation that you use in making your request is as important as what you actually say. When you think someone will refuse your request, you can ask the question in such a way that the refusal does not cause embarrassment.

1. A: Is there any chance of my borrowing your type-writer?

B: For how long?

A: Until the end of the week.

B: Yes, I guess that would be all right.

2. A: Would you mind if I borrowed your car?

B: Well, when exactly?
   A: Until Monday or Tuesday of next week.
   B: I'm sorry, but it's just not possible.

(8) Giving Compliments

Friends often compliment one another on clothes, especially if the clothes are new.

1. A: What a beautiful sweater!
   B: Do you think it looks good on me?
   A: Yes, and it goes beautifully with your pants.
   B: You won't believe it, but it was really cheap.
   A: I wish I could find one just like it.

2. A: I like your new coat.
   B: Do you think it fits OK?
   A: Yes. It looks terrific!
   B: I bought it at half price.
   A: You were lucky to find it.

(9) Apologizing

Sometimes it is necessary to tell someone bad news gently.

1. A: I'm afraid I spilled coffee on the tablecloth.
   B: Oh, don't worry about it.
   A: I want to apologize. Is there anything I can do?
   B: Just forget about it. I never did like it anyway.

2. A: I'm really sorry, but I seem to have misplaced your scarf.
   B: Oh, that's all right.
   A: I'm very sorry. Can I get you another one?
   B: No. Forget about it. It's not important.

(10) Complaining

It's a good idea to be as polite as possible even when complaining about something.

1. A: I wish you wouldn't play the TV so loud.
   B: Sorry. Where you trying to sleep?
   A: Yes. And while I think of it, please ask when you want to borrow my records.
   B: I'm sorry. You're right. I should have asked.

2. A: Do you think you could keep the noise down?

　　B: I'm sorry. Am I keeping you awake?

　　A: Yes. And another thing, would you mind not making long distance calls?

　　B: I'm sorry. I thought you wouldn't mind.

(11) The weather

A very common way to start a conversation is to talk about the weather. When you're traveling, remember that there is considerable variation in climate in the United States.

1. A: Beautiful day, isn't it?

　　B: Yes, it's not like what the radio said at all.

　　A: I wish it would stay this way for the weekend.

　　B: As long as it doesn't snow!

2. A: It seems to be clearing up.

　　B: It's such a nice change.

　　A: I really don't think this weather will last.

　　B: Let's just hope it doesn't get cold again.

(12) Asking for Change

It is sometimes difficult to get change without buying something, so it's a good idea to carry change with you at all times. If you need change, you can buy something inexpensive like candy or a newspaper and ask for the coins you need.

1. A: Excuse me, but could you give me some change?

　　B: Let me see. Are dimes and quarters OK?

　　A: I want to make a long distance phone call.

　　B: Then you'll need small change.

2. A: Sorry to bother you, but do you have change for a one?

　　B: I'll have to look. What do you want it for?

　　A: I need it for the parking meter.

　　B: I can give you quarters, if that'll help.

(13) Making a Telephone Call

The telephone system in the United States, as in many other countries, has a special number for each region of the country. It is called as "area code". If you know the area code and the phone number, it's usually cheaper to dial the number yourself. Of course, you must go through an operator to make person-to-person or collect calls. You can dial direct to many countries overseas or you can ask for the overseas operator.

1. A: Operator.

   B: I'd like to make a collect call to Los Angeles. That's area code 213-486-2435.

   A: And what's the name of the person you want to speak to?

   B: Susan Greene.

2. A: Operator.

   B: Yes, Operator. I'd like to place a person-to-person call to Chicago. The number is 932-8647, but I don't know the area code.

   A: Who do you want to speak to?

   B: I'll speak to anyone at extension 214.

(14) Making a Telephone Call

When using a public telephone, be sure to read the directions carefully before dialing.

1. A: Hello. Can I speak to Yolanda, please?

   B: Hold on, please.

   A: Thank you.

   B: Sorry, but she's out.

   A: Would you tell her Tom Gray called?

   B: I'd be glad to.

2. A: Hello. Is Marie Ward there, please?

   B: I'll see if she's in.

   A: OK.

   B: I'm afraid she's not here.

   A: Could you give her a message, please?

   B: Yes, of course.

(15) Asking for Directions

People are usually helpful when you ask for directions. You should try to have the exact address and be as specific as possible. Telephone directories are the most common source of addresses. Remember that many cities and some towns are built in "blocks". People will often tell you, for example, to "go two blocks and turn right."

1. A: Excuse me, Can you tell me where Main Street is?

    B: Turn left at the second light and then go straight for two blocks.

    A: Is it far?

    B: No. It's only a five-minute walk.

    A: Thanks a lot.

    B: You're welcome.

2. A: Excuse me. Could you please tell me how to get to the station?

    B: Turn left at the first light. You can't miss it.

    A: Will it take me long to get there?

    B: No. It's not far at all.

    A: Thank you.

    B: Don't mention it.

(16) Making an Appointment

It is usually necessary to make an appointment with a doctor, dentist or lawyer. You should call as far in advance as possible.

1. A: Would Dr. Block be able to see me at 9:30 tomorrow?

    B: I'm sorry, but she won't have any openings until 11:00, unless there's a cancellation.

    A: Would 1:00 be convenient?

    B: Yes, she's free then.

2. A: I wonder if the dentist could fit me in early tomorrow?

    B: I'm afraid there's nothing available before noon.

    A: How about 12:45?

    B: Sorry, but she's busy then too.

(17) On a Bus

In cities, buses have letters or numbers indicating their routes. Usually the exact fare is required because you can't get change on a bus. Long-distance travel by bus is common throughout the United States and Canada. It is an inexpensive, scenic way to travel. Special tickets for unlimited travel are sometimes offered by the larger bus companies.

1. A: Does this bus go to the train station?
   B: No, You'll have to get off at the bank and take the A52.
   A: How long is the ride?
   B: About ten minutes.
2. A: Is this the bus for Park Ridge?
   B: No. It only goes as far as Main Street, but you can get the Number 31 there.
   A: How long does it take to get there?
   B: It only takes a few minutes.

(18) Taking a Taxi

Taxi fares vary from city to city. In some cities, taxis have meters that tell you the fare. For long rides, it is a good idea to ask in advance what the approximate fare will be. This is especially true if you're taking a taxi from an airport. You should tip taxi drivers about 15% of the total fare.

1. A: Kennedy Airport, please. I have to be there by 7:00.
   B: I can't promise anything, but I'll do my best.
   B: OK. That'll be $12.00, please.
   A: Thanks a lot. Here.
2. A: Do you think you can get me to Union station by quarter after?
   B: We shouldn't have any trouble if the traffic isn't too heavy.
   B: You've got plenty of time. That's $7.65, please.
   A: Thank you very much. Here's $10.00. Give me $1.00 back, please.

(19) At a Railroad Station

Long-distance travel by train is not as common in the United Stated as it many other parts of the world. Most train travel is in the "Northeast Corridor" linking Boston, New York, Philadelphia, Baltimore and Washington, D.C. Special express trains called "Metroliners" travel between New York and Washington, D.C. All seats on these trains are reserved in both coach(2nd class) and club car(1st class) Long-distance trains also serve major cities such as Atlanta, Miami, New Orleans, Chicago, Los Angeles, San Francisco and Seattle. Sleeping compartments are available on most long-distance trains and must be reserved in advance. Most trains are operated by AMTRAK, the national railroad corporation.

1. A: What time does the train for Boston leave?

    B: 9:25 on Track 12.

    A: When does it arrive?

    B: It should be there at 11:45, but it may be a little late.

    A: How much is a one-way ticket?

    B: It's $32.00 coach and $50.00 club car.

2. A: Which train do I take to Philadelphia?

    B: Track 4 at 9:30.

    A: How long does it take?

    B: It's due in at noon.

    A: What's the round-trip fare?

    B: It's $25.00 one way or $45.00 for a weekend excursion.

(20) The New York City Subway

There are subway systems in several cities in the US. New York City has an extensive and rather complicated rapid transit system. Each train is designated by a letter or a number, but most New Yorkers refer to them by such names as the Broadway Local and the 6th Avenue Express. It is important to remember that both local and express trains operate on some lines. You must have a token or, in some cases, the exact change to get on the platforms. Subway maps are available at most token booths.

1. A: Which train do I take to Columbus Circle, please?

    B: Take the uptown A train and get off at the next station.

    A: And where do I get the train?

    B: Just go down those steps.

2. A: How do I get to Rockefeller Center?

    B: Take the RR to 34th Street, then change to the D train and go two stops.

    A: Which platform is it on?

    B: Go down the stairs over there.

(21) Making Airline Reservations

You can go to a travel agency or talk directly to the airlines to make air travel arrangements. Remember that some cities have more than one airport. Be sure you know which airport and terminal your flight leaves from.

1. A: I want to fly to Chicago on Thursday, the 1st.
   B: Let me see what's available.
   A: I want to go coach, and I'd prefer a morning flight.
   B: United's Flight 102 leaves at 9:20.
   A: That's fine. What time do I have to be at the airport?
   B: Check-in time is 8:45.
2. A: I'd like to make a reservation to Los Angeles for next Monday.
   B: Just a second and I'll check the schedule.
   A: I'll need an economy ticket with an open return.
   B: TWA has a fight leaving at 9:25.
   A: I guess that's OK. What time should I check in?
   B: You have to be there half an hour before departure time.

(22) Renting a Car

It is possible to use a foreign license when driving in the United States, but it is a good idea to have an international driver's license. If you do not have an internationally recognized credit card, a large deposit is usually required to rent a car. Each state has its own driving regulations, so pay close attention to road signs.

1. A: How much is it to rent an economy car?
   B: $19.00 a day or $129.00 a week, unlimited mileage.
   A: Could I have one for tomorrow morning?
   B: Do you have your driver's license?
   A: Sure. Here it is.
   B: Good. Now just complete this form.
2. A: What's the rate for a station wagon?
   B: The daily rate is $32.00 plus 39 Cents per mile.
   A: Good. I'll take it right now, if possible.
   B: Can I see your license, please?
   A: Of course. I have my own license and an international license.
   B: That's fine. Fill out this form and let me see your credit card, please.

(23) At a Gas Station

When you buy gas, you should tell the attendant whether you want unleaded, regular or premium gas. You can either ask for a special amount, such as ten dollar's worth, or you can ask the attendant to "fill it up". If the attendant fills it up, he or she will then tell you how much it comes to.

1. A: Fill it up with unleaded and check the oil, please.

   B: Do you want me to check the tires?

   A: No, that's all for now. What does it come to?

   B: $10.00.

2. A: Fill it up with regular, please.

   B: All right. Should I take a look at your battery?

   A: No, thanks. I'm in a hurry. How much is it?

   B: $10.00, please.

(24) On the Highway

The interstate highway system makes long-distance travel by car fast and convenient. Interstate highways are clearly marked with numbers: odd numbers mark north and south routes and even numbers mark east and west routes. Such toll roads as turnpikes, thruways and parkways are part of the interstate system. The speed limit on all highways is 55 miles per hour unless otherwise posted. Remember that 1 mile=1.6 kilometers.

1. A: We'd better stop and rest pretty soon.

   B: OK. I'll look at the map to see exactly where we are.

   A: Do you think we'll have any trouble finding a room for the night?

   B: I'm sure it'll be easy to find a place.

2. A: We have to watch for Interstate 87?

   B: Right! We still have a ways to go, though.

   A: How about staying at a hotel in a city tonight?

   B: It might be hard to find a good place to stay this late.

(25) At a Hotel

Hotel and motel rates vary considerably. In major cities and resort areas, it is advisable to have reservations.

1. A: Do you have any vacancies?

   B: Yes, we have a nice room on the fourth floor.

  A: How much is it?

  B: $45.00 a night, plus tax.

  A: Can I see it, please?

  B: Certainly. Would you come with me?

2. A: Do you have a single room for two nights?

  B: We only have a small suite.

  A: What's the rate?

  B: $50.00 a night, including breakfast.

  A: Fine. Could you show it to me, please?

  B: Of course. Just follow me.

(26) Finding a Room

In smaller cities and towns, it's usually quite easy to find a room to rent. This is especially true in towns where universities or college are located.

1. A: Do you take in students?

  B: Yes. If you don't mind sharing room, there's one available.

  A: How much is it?

  B: $30.00 a week.

  A: Do you think I could have a look at it, please?

  B: I'm on my way out now. Could you come back in an hour?

2. A: I've been told you might have a vacant room.

  B: Yes. I have a spare room.

  A: How much are you asking?

  B: $10.00 a night.

  A: Could I see the room, please?

  B: Sure. Come on in.

(27) At a Bank

Banking hours are usually from 9:00 to 3:00, Monday to Friday. Sometimes you can't get service in a bank unless you have an account there.

1. A: I'd like to change these pesos, please.

  B: How do you want them?

  A: It doesn't make any difference.

B: Did you want anything else?

   A: Yes, I'd like to open an account.

2. A: Would you cash these travelers checks, please?

   B: How would you like them?

   A: In ten dollar bill, please.

   B: Is there anything else?

   A: Yes, I'd like to know how to send money to France.

(28) In a Post Office

Every mailing address in the United States has a "ZIP code" which should be used whenever possible. Post offices are generally open from 8:30 to 5:00 from Monday to Friday and until noon on Saturday.

1. A: How much is an airmail letter to Japan?

   B: I'll have to check. Can I help you with anything else?

   A: I'd like a 20 cent stamp, please.

   B: There you are.

2. A: Could you tell me how much it would cost to send this to France by regular mail?

   B: I'll look it up. Is there anything else?

   A: Yes. I'd like five airmail stamps.

   B: Here you are.

(29) Getting a Haircut

Many barber shops or hair stylists now cut both men's and women's hair. Prices vary considerably and it's sometimes necessary to make an appointment.

1. A: How do you want it?

   B: Cut it short all over.

   A: Would you like it washed?

   B: No, thank you. It's OK.

2. A: How would you like it?

   B: Trim the back, but leave it long on the sides, please.

   A: Do you want a shampoo?

   B: No, thanks.

(30) Shopping

Clothing sizes are measured differently in the United States from the way they're measured in countries where the metric system is used.

1. A: Are you being helped?
   B: No. What do you have in brown suede jackets, size 40?
   A: The closest I have is a 38.
   B: Do you think you'll be getting any more in?
   A: No, but they might have them at our other store.
2. A: Is anybody waiting on you?
   B: No. I'm trying to find a green sweater in extra large.
   B: We have your size, but not in that color.
   A: Can you order one for me?
   B: Certainly. Just give me your name and address.

(31) Planning an Evening Out (1)

In the United States, girls and boys usually begin to go out on "dates" when they are 14 or 15. Typical dates include going to the movies, going dancing or going to a party.

1. A: How would you like to go to a movie tonight?
   B: Thanks for asking, but I don't think so.
   A: Then what about trying that new Chinese restaurant?
   B: No. I'd rather stay home and watch TV.
2. A: How about going to see Maria tonight?
   B: Not tonight. Maybe another time.
   A: Come on! It would do you good to get out.
   B: No. I want to get to bed early tonight.

(32) Planning an Evening Out (2)

It's OK to make plans with friends at the last minute. It's more polite, however, to make them ahead of time.

1. A: How about going to hear a country-and-western singer tonight?
   B: I'd enjoyed that.
   A: I' pick you up around 8:00.
   B: OK. I'll see you then.

2. A: Do you feel like going to see Paul and Claire tonight?

   B: I'd like that very much.

   A: How does 7:30 sound?

   B: Fine. See you late.

(33) Buying Theater Tickets

Going to the theater is very popular and shows are often sold out far in advance. It is a good idea to buy your tickets in advance if you want to see a particular show. It is not necessary to tip the person who shows you to your seat in a theater.

1. A: I'd like to reserve two seats for tomorrow night.

   B: Would you like orchestra seats?

   A: Isn't there anything less expensive?

   B: Not unless you want the matinee.

2. A: Can I still get tickets for tonight's performance?

   B: The front balcony is still available.

   A: Aren't there any other seats?

   B: No, I'm afraid that's it.

(34) Watching Television

There are three nationwide television networks in the United States: the American Broadcasting Company(ABC), the Columbia Broadcasting Company(CBS) and the National Broadcasting Company(NBC) There is also a public broadcasting network(PBS), and there are hundreds of local television stations. In many areas television is broadcast 24 hours a day.

1. A: Is there anything worth watching on another channel?

   B: I think there's a western on.

   A: Do you mind if we watch it? I'd really like to see it.

   B: Well, I really wanted to see the baseball game.

2. A: Do you happen to know what's on after the news?

   B: I've got a feeling there's a documentary about animals.

   A: Does anybody mind if we watch it?

   B: Don't you want to see part two of the movie?

(35) Sports

Both team sports and individual sports are extremely popular in the United States. Don't be afraid to try a sport you haven't played before. People are usually willing to help beginners.

1. A: Would you like to go running?
   B: I'd enjoy that. Where would you like to go?
   A: We could go to the park. There shouldn't be many people there now.
   B: Good. Just let me change.
2. A: How about going for a bike ride?
   B: Sure. Where?
   A: Let's call Harry and ask him. He always knows the best places to go.
   B: That's a good idea. I'll get ready.

(36) At Breakfast

Coffee shops are popular, reasonably priced restaurants for breakfast, lunch, dinner or just a snack.

1. A: You're having coffee, aren't you?
   B: Yes, I always have coffee in the morning.
   A: What are you going to have to eat?
   B: I'm going to order scrambled eggs and toast. What about you?
   A: That sounds good to me. I'll have the same.
2. A: You'd like coffee, wouldn't you?
   B: I think I'd rather have tea this morning.
   A: What else are you going to have?
   B: Just an English muffin. What are you going to have?
   A: That sounds good. I'm going to order the same thing.

(37) At Lunch

Lunch is usually served between noon and 2:00. Sandwiches are a very popular quick lunch in both the United States and Canada.

1. A: Please have another sandwich.
   B: Thank you, but I really can't eat any more.
   A: You're going to have dessert, aren't you?
   B: Well, I'll join you if you're having something.

2. A: You'll finish the chicken, won't you?

B: No, thank you. I'm trying to cut down.

A: Aren't you going to have dessert?

B: No, thank you. I just can't eat any more.

(38) At Dinner

Dinner time varies somewhat in the United States. In small towns it may be as early as 5:00, while in large cities it may be as late as 9:00. It's best to call for a reservation in expensive or well-known restaurants.

1. A: Would you like to order now?

    B: Yes. I'll have the shrimp cocktail to start.

    A: What would you like for your main course?

    B: I'll have a sirloin steak, medium rare.

2. A: May I take your order?

    B: Yes. I'd like a cup of onion soup.

    A: And what would you like after that?

    B: I'd like the roast chicken, please.

(39) At Fast Food Restaurant

Fast food restaurants are popular in the United States for quick, inexpensive meals or snacks. You order your food and take it to a table yourself. If you order your food "to go", you take it out of the restaurant. Tipping is not necessary in this kind of restaurant.

1. A: What would you like to eat?

    B: I'd like a hamburger with lettuce and tomato.

    A: How about something to drink?

    B: A Coke, please.

    A: OK. I'll see if I can get waited on.

2. A: What do you want?

    B: I think I'll have a piece of apple pie.

    A: Do you want something to drink?

    B: Coffee would be fine.

    A: OK. Sit down and I'll get it.

(40) At a Cocktail Party

Cocktail parties are popular for both business and social functions. They may be casual or formal and are often held between 6:00 and 8:00 in the evening. Drinks and hors d'oeuvres or snacks are usually served.

1. A: Come in. It's nice to see you again.
　B: It's nice to be here.
　A: Would you care for a drink?
　B: Just a club soda for me, please.
2. A: Hi! I'm happy you could make it.
　B: Well, I've been looking forward to seeing you.
　A: What can I get you?
　B: I'd love a gin and tonic.

(41) Asking About Health

People often ask about health out of politeness. This is a very common way to begin a conversation.

1. A: How's your father been?
　B: He's been out of work for a couple of days.
　A: What's wrong with him?
　B: He has a bad cold.
　A: Well, tell him to take it easy and that I hope he feels better.
　B: Thanks. I'll tell him.
2. A: Where's Tony this evening?
　B: He's a little under the weather.
　A: Really! What's the matter with him?
　B: He has the flu.
　A: Tell him I was asking about him.
　B: I will.

42) At the doctors

It's usually best to go to a doctor that someones has recommended. In an emergency, you should go directly to the emergency entrance of the nearest hospital. Medical services in the United States are generally very expensive.

1. A: I have a sore throat and my chest hurts.

   B: How long have you been like this?

   A: Two or three days now.

   B: I think you've got the flu. There's a lot of it going around.

   A: What do you think I ought to do?

   B: Get this prescription filled and go straight to bed.

2. A: I have the chills and an upset stomach.

   B: How long have you felt like this?

   A: For most of the week.

   B: It sounds as if you have a virus.

   A: What do you think I should do?

   B: I'll give you something. I want you to take it easy and come back in a couple of days.

(43) At the Dentist's Office

Dental work is usually quite expensive. Appointments are usually made far in advance, but many dentists will try to fit you if you have an urgent problem.

1. A: How long have you felt like this?

   B: It started bothering me yesterday afternoon.

   A: I think I'd better take an X-ray.

   B: Can you see anything?

   A: It's a small cavity. It should be easy to fill.

2. A: When did your toothache start?

   B: It's been this way for a few days.

   A: Let me take a look at it.

   B: What do you think?

   A: You're got an abscess. I don't think we can save the tooth.

(44) At a Drugstore

If you are taking medication regularly, you should take what you need with you when you travel. You should also bring a copy of any prescription that you are taking since many drugs are only available by prescription. Drugstores, or pharmacies, sell cosmetics and toiletries as well as many other products.

1. A: I'd like to have this prescription filled.
   B: It'll only take a few minutes if you want to wait.
   A: Have you got something for chapped lips?
   B: Rub this cream on every four hours.
2. A: Could you fill this prescription for me, please?
   B: I'll take care of it right away.
   A: By the way, what do you suggest for insect bites?
   B: This ointment should help.

(45) At a restaurant

A: It's very nice of you to invite me.

B: I'm very glad you could come, Mr. Liu. Will you take a seat at the head of the table? It's an informal dinner, please don't stand on ceremony... Mr. Liu, would you like to have some chicken?

A: Thank you. This is my first time to come to a Chinese restaurant. Could you tell me the different features of Chinese food?

B: Generally speaking, Cantonese food is a bit light; Shanghai food is rather oily; and Hunan dishes are very spicy, having a strong and hot taste.

A: Chinese dishes are exquisitely prepared, delicious, and very palatable. They are very good in colour, flavour, and taste.

B: Mr. liu, would you care for another helping?

A: No more, thank you. I'm quite full.

B: Did you enjoy the meal?

A: It's the most delicious dinner I've had for a long time. It's such a rich dinner.

B: I'm so glad you like it.

A: Thank you very much for your hospitality

(46) Shopping

A: I would like to buy a bottle of cleansing milk. Can you recommend me some kinds?

B: Sure. What kind of skin do you have?

A: My skin is oily.

B: Then I advise you to buy the OLAY cleansing milk.

A: Can you tell me more?

(47) Asking the way

A: Pam, where's the closest ATM?

B: It's not that far. Do you see that Yellow building over there?

A: The big one or the small one?

B: The big one.

A: Yes.

B: It's right next to it, on the right.

A: Do you know if there's a convenience store around here?

B: I don't think there's one around here. The closest one is on 3rd street, but that's probably closed now.

A: I really need to get some things before I leave.

B: Well, you could go down to 22nd street. There are lot of stores down there that are open 24 hours a day.

A: Can I take the subway to get there?

B: Yes, but that'll probably take about half an hour. You should just take a cab.

A: Won't that be expensive?

B: No, from here I think it's only about 5 dollars.